P9-DEJ-931

Risks & Rewards

Risks AND Rewards

A MEMOIR

JULIA MONTGOMERY WALSH

in collaboration with

ANNE CONOVER CARSON

Library of Congress Cataloging-in-Publication Data
Walsh, Julia Montgomery.
          Risks and Rewards: A Memoir/Julia Montgomery Walsh
in collaboration with Anne Conover Carson.—1st ed.
          p. cm.

Includes index.
ISBN 0-939009-98-6
1. Walsh, Julia Montgomery.
2. Stockbrokers—United States—Biography.
3. Women in finance—New York (State)—New York—Biography.
1. Carson, Anne Conover, 1937–
HG4621 .W34A3 1996
332.63'22'092—dc20

96-17593
CIP

[B]
Copyright © 1996 by Julia Walsh
All rights reserved
EPM Publications, Inc., 1003 Turkey Run Road, McLean, Virginia 22101
Printed in the United States of America
Design: Lisa Carey

Contents

A Few Words About
Julia Montgomery Walsh

When *Wall $treet Week With Louis Rukeyser*
first went on television in 1970, Wall Street was arguably
the most chauvinistic profession in America. But a few bold
female pioneers had already been knocking down the sexist
doors, and none more notably than Julia Montgomery
Walsh, who—when she gained entry to the American Stock
Exchange in 1965—became the first woman member of
a major stock exchange.

At a time when too many women were frightened away
from investing because arrogant men told them they lacked the
ability and/or the funds, Julia offered both inspiration and
encouragement. As she herself said, in one of her memorable
appearances on our program, "You can start accumulating
with a hundred dollars in your pocket—the mutual funds are
a small investment—if you do this intelligently and don't
try to pretend you're a big wheeler-dealer. Brokerage houses
today can't handle the $2,000 wheeler-dealers, but they're not
upset about handling the $2,000 *accumulator*. There's a vast
difference. The minute you start, you're an *accumulator*-
investor, then you become an *investor*-investor when you graduate with enough money and enough experience to move on."

Julia's simple common sense, combined with remarkable financial astuteness and a warm personality, quickly made her a favorite with viewers—and with me personally. After she scored initial success as a guest, we made her a member of our revolving panel. She was the first woman to be so selected and a marvelous role model for the many women who have followed as panelists on *Wall $treet Week With Louis Rukeyser.*

One personal story may give an insight into Julia's special humility. At our fifteenth anniversary program in 1985, my late father (then 88 years old) was paying Julia some well-deserved compliments. "Thank you," she said, "but now they have so many other women on the program who are younger, prettier and smarter." My father hesitated not an instant before replying: "I don't agree with even two-thirds of that statement!"

And Julia's influence lives on in the '90s. On March 27, 1992, I had the honor of inducting Julia as the first woman member of "The *Wall $treet Week With Louis Rukeyser* Hall of Fame." It was an honor she richly deserves, and I hope she will continue to inspire young investors—female and male—for many years to come. Julia Montgomery Walsh is truly a blue-chip human being.

Louis Rukeyser

A Few Words…

Introduction

When I first met Julia Montgomery Walsh and heard her speak, I was awed—as was the rest of her audience—with her charisma. She is a tall woman, with striking white hair, strong, handsome features, and vivid blue eyes that look directly at you, very different from the stuffy, self-important Wall-Street types. Her throaty, resonant voice commanded attention; the way she carried herself, the way she dressed, inspired confidence and let people know that she "meant business," that she herself was doing well.

You may have seen her on *Wall $treet Week With Louis Rukeyser*, and on any list of the most successful women in the financial world, Julia Montgomery Walsh has stood out as bigger than life. Her colleagues admire her, not only because she parlayed a small nest egg into a fortune of several million dollars, but because of the outstanding way she handled her personal life. How many women can be a loving wife, successful role model and mother to *twelve* children and step-children, while not missing a beat in a high-pressure, demanding job? Julia is the quintessential woman who has had it all—an important career, a husband, *and* children.

The list of Julia's career achievements as a pathfinder in a man's world is long, and I shall highlight here only a few milestones:

> *First woman to be admitted to the Institute of Investment Banking at the Wharton School.*
>
> *First woman to be accepted by the Advanced Management Program at Harvard University.*
>
> *First woman to serve on the Board of Governors of the American Stock Exchange.*
>
> *One of only three women in the U.S. to head her own investment firm.*

What were the special strengths of character that made Julia a success? She was born a "cock-eyed optimist," in her own words. Though she had some bad times—everyone does—she had faith in the future and always bounced back. Even in early correspondence that she never imagined would be read by anyone but family, there emerges a spiritual quality and a strong Catholic faith that sustained her when the going got rough. According to friends and family, she is generous to a fault with her time and money. This explains, in part, why the friendships of her youth lasted a lifetime.

Was she, as she appeared to many at first meeting, born with the traditional silver spoon in her mouth? In Julia's own words, "I came from a background where *everything I had, I built myself...*starting from ground zero." The most important element seemed to be risk-taking: "Putting your reputation and future on the line, in an attempt to do something *bigger* and *better*." [Julia's words] In her view, this applied to anyone striving for more out of life, no matter what the career.

Was it Herculean hard work, risk-taking, timing, or just plain luck—or a combination of the above—that put Julia on top? Just making money was never her primary goal, though she made a pile of it as a reward for her efforts. "I wanted to see whether, in my lifetime, I could put together something meaningful in the world of business; I was curious to see whether it could be done by a *woman*."

As Julia's story unfolds, we shall see that her life is important, not because of *how big* she made it, but because of *how well* she did it. It will prove to younger women trying to make it in the formerly all-male bastion of business, that Julia is not Superwoman, she is EVERYWOMAN WRIT LARGE!

Anne Conover Carson

Julia Montgomery Walsh

Margaret Julia Curry ("Peggy"), born March 29, 1923, would later be called Julia. Here she is with her brother Edward.

CHAPTER ONE

Peggy Curry Goes To Washington

As a girl growing up in a traditional working-class Catholic family in Mid-America, Margaret Julia Curry was expected to be a God-fearing dutiful daughter, a useful human being, but not destined for great deeds. Akron, Ohio, was a company town, and my father, Ed Curry, like most of the men I knew, spent 33 years on the assembly line, bringing home a paycheck from the Goodyear Tire and Rubber Company. My mother, Catherine ("Kate") Curry, was in many ways a woman ahead of her time. She worked as a bookkeeper in the Goodyear plant until she married, all the while using her good mind to continue her education at home. She was an avid reader, and I discovered the joy of reading early in life. Sitting down with a book was accepted family behavior.

During the Great Depression of the 1930s, Mother was a genius at stretching Dad's paycheck so that we never did without anything we needed, creating a comfortable home for my brother, Ed Jr., and me. My parents always expected "Peggy," their young daughter, to be just as good at everything as her brother, who was two years older. He was a hard act to follow, and I kept stretching to keep up with him. You might say I was a tomboy. Even as a child I used to play at business in my "office," instead of pretending to be a school teacher or a nurse like other little girls of my generation.

As I look back, there was a continuing pattern of leadership in my life, but it just happened—there wasn't any grand plan or design. You can tell by the 1935 school photo of me with the Peter Pan collar, the short dark hair and the big smile, I was not a spectacular beauty. I was a serious girl who made good grades, and my greatest assets were an outgoing personality and an ability to organize and to work with people.

Early on, I had an opportunity to do both. I joined one of the Midget Clubs, to my knowledge the only groups of their kind in the U.S. at that time. The Midgets were initiated by the Junior Federation of Women's Clubs in Akron for the purpose of grooming young girls for future organization work. With my classmates Henrietta Carrell, Janice Waugh, Phyllis Miley, and Betty Coburn, I helped to plan the Midgets' first flower show, held at the local YWCA. (The Akron *Beacon-Journal* reported that Miss Margaret Curry was Chairman of Entries.) Before long, I was elected president of Xi Club, an affiliate of the Midget Federation. My mother, one of the sponsors and a member of the Goodyear Women's Club, was very proud when we attended meetings of the County Federation together. But it wasn't all work and no play. I also helped to organize the Midgets' mid-summer picnic at Metropolitan Park, with games and a program of silly stunts and songs.

When I graduated from the Midgets, it was time for Akron's East High School. As an extra-curricular activity, I joined the string section of the school orchestra, but being a left-handed violin player, I was out of sync with the rest of the group. The conductor suggested I take up the French horn. I joined the marching band and was very proud to be "stepping out" in a scarlet and gray uniform with bright brass buttons at the East High football games.

I began to take an active part in student government, another opportunity for leadership. As a girl competing against the odds-on favorite, Lawson Dunn, I was the surprise candidate elected president of the East High Student Council. Presidents from all the Akron-area high schools automatically became members of the Intra-City Student Council, and when there was a conference in another part of the state, we had opportunities to meet other young people from many different areas. Soon I was elected president of the Intra-City Council. When the then-Superintendent of Schools, Ralph Waterhouse, met with local high school officers and principals, he called the Council a "molder of better citizens." In my case, it certainly was true. At East High, I had my first taste of the rewards of leadership and public service. (Fortunately, my mother saved a scrapbook of these events to refresh my memory.)

On Commencement Day, June 11, 1941, I was Salutatorian of my class and winner of the Award for Citizenship. When I walked down the aisle of the Akron Armory with the Honor Winners—among the High Ten—my proud parents were there to cheer me on. Our class motto was: "He who climbs may have a fall; but better a fall than not to climb at all." I always remember that.

❧ II

Ed Curry was a kind man, a good father, but he didn't see any reason for his girl to go to college. The plant was gearing up for World War II. As a hard-working assembler in the airplane tire division, he thought his daughter should learn to type and get a job helping out with the war effort, earning good money like my other young friends.

But my strong-minded mother had other ideas. She did not want her bright and independent daughter to be limited

Peggy Curry Goes To Washington

by a life in hometown Akron, as she had been. In our family, there was never enough money. She encouraged me to apply for a scholarship to Smith College, where my horizons would be broader than the blue skies of Ohio. I had never strayed far from the industrial city of some 200,000 where I was born, but I dreamed of the well-kept lawns of a New England campus, where girls with long "page-boy" hair, shetland sweater-sets and saddle shoes would share my dormitory and my new life.

This was not to be. I won the scholarship, but it did not include transportation. Northampton, Massachusetts was a long way from Akron, Ohio. There were wartime restrictions on travel and, to make it worse, my father refused to lend me the money for whatever train trips I could take to Smith. I lost that battle; it never occurred to me to fight with him. In those days, good Catholic girls did what their fathers told them to do; we did not fight back.

My mother fought for me, however, and they compromised. Kent State University was only eleven miles east of Akron. Mother sent for an application, which noted that "students may find modern facilities and a scholarly faculty within a few miles of their home." In my case, it meant a long, hard commute by the Penn-Ohio rail and bus system, but I could live with my parents and help to pay college expenses. In those days, Ohio residents could attend the state-supported school by paying a registration fee of $20 per quarter, a health fee of $1.75, and a $3.75 activities fee! The only other costs were books, the noon meal, and transportation—the most expensive item. By the end of the first year, I had earned some $1,000 of my expenses. I used my talent for speaking and a sense of humor to become a popular lecturer at local Democratic women's clubs.

In 1942 I founded the Office of War Activities, which directed the War Chest drive on campus, good training for future fund-raising. Among other extra-curricular activities during my four years at Kent State were the Cardinal Key, a national women's honorary society, Zeta Iota, the honorary society for women in business, and the Young Women's Christian Association, of which I was vice president.

I was also president of the International Relations Club. The summer of my sophomore year, I was selected by Dr. K.C. Leebrick, then-president of Kent State, as one of 25 undergraduates from universities throughout the country to study world problems at the International Student Service Summer Training Institute. It was my first time away from home, and the mountains around Asheville, North Carolina (near the Vanderbilt estate, "Biltmore") were a spectacular change from the flat, Midwestern city of Akron. The highlight of the four-week seminar was a visit from Mrs. Eleanor Roosevelt, touring the area in one of her tireless efforts to boost wartime morale and report back to the President on conditions throughout the country. After she addressed our group, I had an opportunity to speak with her face-to-face and to shake her hand. This chance meeting was to change the course of my life.

Peggy Curry's first meeting with First Lady Eleanor Roosevelt.

Something of Mrs. Roosevelt's far-sighted idealism must have rubbed off on me. Back at Kent State, I wrote my term paper on "Post-War Aviation," then a fledgling industry. It was dedicated "to all those people who strive so hard for a solution to the world's problems," and underscored my belief "in the ability of the world's leaders to find at least a partial answer to the threats of peace, one that will serve…until the world has come to think of itself as one great, inter-dependent unit." It ended with an optimistic tribute "to all those who envision this great end…[their] accomplishments shall result in a better world for all of us. Long live the post-war planners!"

In the fall, I was elected student-body president, the first woman in Kent State's history to hold that job (possibly because it was wartime, and many of the talented men were away). The men make more money after graduation, too, I reasoned. The male-dominated field of business always interested me, because that's where the action is—if I was going to work to earn my own living, then I wanted to be well paid. I decided to enroll in the College of Business Administration.

I had to get a job during summer vacations, and the Goodyear plant was the obvious place to apply. My favorite teacher, Professor K.C. Kochendorfer, sent the names of his most promising students in the Motion and Time Study course to the plant manager, and M.J. Curry's name headed the list. I was hired because of my outstanding qualifications on paper, but the day I arrived on the job the irate factory boss sent me home. It was unheard of, in those days, to send a woman to the factory floor! Dr. Kochendorfer was not to be defeated. He phoned back the manager to insist that his top student be allowed to observe Motion and Time (productivity) first-hand on the assembly line. I had no idea then how useful this training would be in the future, managing a business and a large family while juggling social life with civic responsibilities. But I knew I was off and running with a headstart on my career.

The summer between Junior and Senior years (1944), like so many other young hopefuls, I left home for New York to look for a job. I thought I might find a junior executive position in the Big Apple, but was lucky to be hired by W.R. Grace

Shipping Lines on Hanover Square as a clerk in the traffic-booking department—for the munificent salary of $25 for 40-hours work!

My mother went to New York with me for a so-called "vacation." I knew she wanted to see for herself that I was comfortably and safely settled. I didn't resent this; she and I always had a good time together. We rode double-decker buses up Fifth Avenue to Central Park, took in Rockefeller Center and all of the tourist sights before she left for home.

The parents of Ed Sweeney, a friend I met at a Bethany College student conference, were spending the summer at the Long Island shore. They offered to sublet their apartment to me and several of my friends for a modest rent. Dorothy Case, another Ohio girl in New York for the summer, Dale Hinton, and Jane Durivage were my roommates. Sutton Hall on Anscon Avenue in Forest Hills, Long Island, was a posh address for four young girls from the Middle West. We had an eye-opening experience observing how the other half lives.

The Sweeneys treated me like a daughter, and often invited me to their summer place at Point Lookout for weekends. I was determined to keep Ed as just "a friend." I was not ready to marry and settle down yet. My parents' partnership was my ideal of a successful marriage, and I had not yet met anyone who fit the pattern.

My goal for the summer was to get some experience in the business world and to save at least $100 toward my college expenses—a lot of money in those days—while having a great time in the Big City. I reported to work at 9 A.M., got off at 5 P.M. weekdays, Saturdays at noon. There were four of us in the office, but I had my own private desk, an unusual feature for a new girl on the block. We booked cargo onto every Grace Line ship leaving New York harbor. It was very busy when a steamer was in port, but there were long lulls with nothing doing when I could catch up on my personal correspondence.

Peggy Curry Goes To Washington

(I was a faithful letter writer in those days, almost daily to my parents, plus many friends in the service overseas).

I liked my job because it kept me in touch with all types of people, many of them South Americans, whom I had not known before. I was surprised to discover that the management of the Grace Company was predominantly Catholic. It appeared to me that their policies toward employees were more humanitarian than most. They offered a free beverage and dessert at lunchtime, free hospitalization, and two weeks vacation with pay, plus a cost-of-living increase at the end of one year. I was tempted to stay on to take advantage of the many benefits!

I have always had more than my share of energy. As if I didn't have enough to do commuting to work, after a week or so I enrolled in a "Shipping for Trade" course at Columbia University, to make better use of the evenings. (I considered working in the cafeteria to pay for my evening meal, but even I couldn't stretch my strength and enthusiasm that far.)

In spite of my good record at Kent State, I had to struggle to keep up with the competition of my classmates at Columbia, most of whom came from competitive Eastern prep schools and colleges. By some miracle and constant prayer, I passed the course and won the accolade of my professor on the final night: "The Middle West can be proud of you, Miss Curry." I celebrated with a class party and an open-air taxi ride along the Hudson River with my classmate, Ed Stefrak.

There were many other diversions that summer. In spite of the fact that it was the hottest on record for 60 years, we walked from the office to Times Square, enjoyed the concerts in Central Park and other enticements of the Big Apple. I attended a CBS broadcast starring then-famous Jessica Dragonette, and viewed a current Broadway hit, "The Searching Wind." I took comfort in praying for my brother and the other boys fighting overseas and thanking God for my many blessings at majestic St. Patrick's Cathedral.

When my classmate Hilder Coons came to visit, we discovered a spaghetti restaurant in Greenwich Village with "all you can eat" for 30 cents! Since it was wartime, there were food shortages. We scrimped to send ration points home to our parents. We created imaginative menus with meat loaf and invited service men from the Catholic USO to share our Sunday dinners with us.

There was a constantly revolving door at our Long Island sublet. While Ed Sweeney was away in the service, his brother and an ensign friend came for parties on weekends and escorted Dot and me around New York. When I first came to the Big City, I was still "pinned" to George Glamack, a Beta from North Carolina. (I could not understand why he was angry when I accepted a pin from a rival Sigma Chi, in my view depriving me of the pleasures of youth.) I went up to Harvard for an "intellectual" weekend in August. I visited the Merchant Marine Academy with Bill, who had landed with the Marines at Tarawa.

My friend Webb (Webster Colfield III), a Ph.D. at the University of Chicago, proved his devotion by corresponding faithfully every week from the Faculty Club on the very original "Cash and *Curry*" letterhead he designed. (At the time, I wrote to my mother, "He and I are so right for each other— he may be *the* one!")

My parents despaired that I would ever settle down, they hoped in Akron. They were still waiting for my brother Ed to come on leave from India, where he was flying planes over the Hump. In September, in spite of the glamorous life I had been living for the past three months, I decided "there's no place like home." I wrote a letter to the parents—signed for the last time, "from your little girl in the Big City"—and headed for Ohio.

Another highlight of my college years was the Conference of Student Body Presidents at the American University in Washington, D.C. Mrs. Roosevelt addressed our group and was especially encouraging to the young women in the audience. Her message was, "Just because you're female, don't tell me you can't do it!" My friend Hilder Coons, an equally tall and husky girl, and I were selected as guides to assist the President's wife in making her way around the campus, running interference through the crowds of enthusiastic students. When I reminded her of our meeting in North Carolina, the First Lady had not forgotten it. She asked if we were enjoying seeing the sights on our first visit to Washington?

"Not yet, Mrs. Roosevelt. We haven't had time to see anything. Every day we've been tied up in meetings, and we can't afford to stay over. Tomorrow, the bus is taking us back to Akron."

"I'll see what I can do to change that," said Mrs. Roosevelt. "How would you and your friend like to come and stay with me at the White House?"

I suspected the First Lady would forget the casual invitation. Mrs. Roosevelt must be too busy to bother with us, I reasoned, she has so many official duties. But the next morning, a long black limousine with chauffeur in full uniform arrived at the University dorm to pick us up and deliver us to the President's House.

I had to let my parents know that we were staying over, so I sent a message by Western Union:

"Not returning on bus. Don't worry. If you need to reach me, call the White House. Love, Peggy."

Imagine Ed Curry's surprise. He thought the telegram was a prank of his "crazy" daughter! That evening, he rang up the White House to check, quite sure he would not reach Peggy Curry at that number.

"One moment, sir," a crisp-voiced operator replied. "Is this an emergency, sir? Miss Curry is dining with Mrs. Roosevelt. Shall I interrupt them?"

The next morning, before my friend and I started out on a sight-seeing tour of the Mall—the Smithsonian Institution, the Capitol and houses of Congress—the upstairs maid in starched uniform knocked on our door, carrying the breakfast trays. Not long after, the First Lady herself stopped by for a chat.

There was Eleanor Roosevelt, looking even more sympathetic than in her photographs, like an older sister sitting at the foot of my bed—the same four-postered bed in which Abraham Lincoln had slept! I thought I had died and gone to heaven. My idol and role model, chatting with me about "my day," inquiring about my hopes, my dreams, my ambitions. What great good luck for 20-year-old Peggy Curry, to visit with the First Lady in this historic place. It surpassed my most ambitious dreams.

At the end of that eventful day, Hilder and I soaked our Mall-blistered feet and our tired-to-the-bone bodies in the President's swimming pool. FDR was at Hot Springs, Georgia, at the time of our visit. I was never to meet the President. On my next visit to Washington—and I still remember the exact date, April 12, 1945—I stood sadly on the corner of Pennsylvania Avenue (where the J.W. Marriott Hotel is today) watching as the caisson moved slowly along, carrying the body of our beloved President to the Capitol, there to lie in state.

⚜III

After meeting Eleanor Roosevelt, I wanted to follow in her footsteps. The idea of public service appealed to me. I finished all my courses and decided to get a three-months head start on my career before Commencement at Kent State. In March

Peggy Curry Goes To Washington

1945 I handed over the gavel of student government to the vice president, Don Wargowsky. I regretted leaving my friends of the past four years, but I took the train to Washington with great expectations. My goal was an overseas post with the Foreign Service.

The parents of a Kent State friend, Ginny Dodds, offered me a spare room with private bath for a modest rent in their comfortable family home at 4371 Lee Highway in Arlington, Virginia. Arlington was then a quiet, shady suburb of Washington. It was a long commute over Key Bridge to my job, but Mr. Dodds dropped me off a half-block from my office every morning on his way to work. I ate the evening meal with the Dodds, and they treated me like their own daughter who was away from home, married to an Army man.

On weekends, when I looked tired and overworked, they took me to their weekend retreat on the Severn River near Chesapeake Bay. I never failed to sleep like a log for 12 hours every night. Another new experience was to go crabbing. Cracking the crab shells and prying them open to pick out the succulent meat was a rare treat for an Ohio girl.

I completed the paper work and interviewed with Personnel at the Department of State. A sympathetic woman took a shine to me, and when I told her I was particularly interested in the Cultural Cooperation division, she said she would take that into consideration when handing out assignments.

My first job was assistant in the Foreign Service Personnel Office, helping to dispatch FSOs to their posts overseas. The first week, I processed papers to Calcutta, Cairo, Zurich and Madrid. We also administered tests and collected data on Vice Consuls all over the world. My beginning salary was $185 per month, out of which I expected to buy a $25 war bond each payday and still *save* $40! (Mine was not an unusual government salary in 1945; my boss Henry Covins, 35-years-old with 12 years of experience, was making only $4,000 a year!)

My office was in what is now the Old Executive Office Building, a turn-of-the-century behemoth which once housed the combined offices of the Departments of State, War and Navy—a bustling beehive of bureaucrats and Army-Navy officers. On one of my first lunch breaks, I was exploring the building and an old guard showed me into the room that had been World War I General John J. Pershing's office. Another day, I stopped by the office of then-Secretary of State Edward Stettinius, who was in San Francisco attending the early meetings of the United Nations. When I peeked into the reception room, a young man showed me around the inner sanctum and afterwards invited me to lunch. He introduced himself as Joseph Borda, the Secretary's personal secretary (recently released from the Navy), who had worked with Stettinius at U.S. Steel before the war. Sometime later, I was among the chosen few invited to hear Ambassador Joseph C. Grew address a group of young FSOs (Foreign Service Officers) in the Diplomatic Reception Rooms.

After I started to work, a new law was passed allowing all government employees Saturdays off after 1 PM. I used this extra time to explore Washington and to meet new friends in the nation's capital—then capital of the free world. I sat in on sessions of the Senate and House, visited the Congressional Library, the Mellon Art Gallery (newly established in the 1940s). I attended concerts on the barge on the banks of the Potomac at the old Watergate on Saturday nights.

Several weekends I traveled to Chester, Pennsylvania to visit my father's brother, Uncle Jim Curry, his wife Lillian and their two daughters. Another cousin, Edna (Aunt Julia Ondach's daughter), was an officer in the WACs, stationed at Bolling Field. If either of us was homesick, we could get together to exchange the latest gossip and memories of the family in Ohio.

But it was an exciting time to be in Washington. In a walk past the White House, one might see President Harry Truman and his entourage zipping by enroute to a summit meeting in Berlin! (After hearing him speak, I knew that Truman would never take the place of my hero, Franklin Delano Roosevelt. In a letter home, I commented that "destiny plays a funny game.")

V-E Day came at last in May. With the recognition that the war was far from over, it was a solemn occasion in Washington. The store windows were beautifully decorated. One I remember had a mammoth sketch of FDR, the wartime President. But unlike New York, there was little public merriment. I went to confession and communion for my own private celebration, praying for FDR, God rest his soul, my brother and other close friends who might soon return home and not have to go overseas again. (For several weeks, my parents had had no word from Ed, still in India.)

My "steady" beau, 6'2" All-American basketball star George Glamack, arrived for the weekend very much in love and wanting to marry me. (My kids later called him "The Blind Bomber." His poor eyesight was a family joke. To explain why he was so crazy about me, they said he couldn't see the basket from the foul line!) On this visit, George presented me with an ultimatum: "Now, or never!" I didn't want to hurt him, and after I calmed him down, I postponed the issue. I thought then and now that every girl should earn her own living before launching out into marriage. "I have absolutely NO intention of being a career woman," I wrote to my parents, "this working for a living is strictly for *men*—but I might as well be a success while I'm at it." Besides, there were many other fish in the sea.

I went to "hops" and June Week at the Naval Academy in Annapolis with my new friend, Midshipman Mel Rogers. We checked out a sailboat on the Chesapeake Bay on a sunny day with a clear blue sky, one of the biggest thrills of my life. Mel gave me a Navy Anchor for remembrance, but how could I ever forget? Walking on the beautiful grounds of the Academy to the Navy Chapel, with some 3,000 Middies marching along singing "Onward, Christian Soldiers," is a memory that still sends chills up my spine.

I had my first experience as hostess to a large group of servicemen—some gentlemen, some not—at the Officers' Candidate Dances at Fort Belvoir. There were dates with a Californian who spoke Arabic, French, German and Russian. And a *Cabot* from Boston, an engineer in Officers' Candidate School, who took me for a canoe trip up the river to the Jefferson Memorial (with intelligent conversation all along the way). And a Ph.D. from Yale in Metallurgy, who invited me to one of the seafood restaurants on the banks of the Potomac. I was flattered by his attentions, but decided (at that time in my life) that he was *too* intelligent and mature for me!

A member of the crew that flew General Williams (of the 9th Troop Carrier Command) was eager to share his first night back from overseas with a "typical American girl." We took a taxi ride past the monuments of Washington, ate donuts, burgers and coffee at the Hot Shoppe, and played pinball machines at the Officers' Club. Our date ended with a handshake and an enthusiastic salute: "Tonight, we've shared the American Heritage!"

My parents despaired that I would ever marry, but I reminded them: though I was not quite ready for wedded bliss, being 22 and single isn't such a hopeless state! I was enjoying my work. Our division was representative of the whole country: my best friends were from California, Wisconsin, Tennessee and Kentucky. I was becoming an important little cog to the big wheel of my division, my boss Henry Covins, coordinating the work of 21 clerks, which led to sure promotion.

About that time, Dr. Fox, head of Cultural Relations, singled me out to inquire if I were interested in going overseas. (I didn't tell him that I was determined to go, not as a clerk but as a Vice Consul or at the very least, Administrative Assistant!)

With that in mind, I enrolled in a Procedures course, and earned an "Excellent" rating. With some German blood in my veins, I was also studying to "sprechen Deutsch." As if I didn't have enough to do in my spare time, I got a Saturday sales job in the book department of the Woodward & Lothrop department store at 11th and F Streets in downtown Washington. It improved my sales skills, but was hell on my feet!

There was one obstacle in my upward path, a highly competitive examination, which I was not at all sure I could pass. I shall never forget the cold, rainy morning I boarded the bus to a battleship-gray government office on the Mall to join several hundred other young hopefuls with sweaty palms taking the 14-hour, two-day exam. I stood on solid ground until I got to the questions on the geography, history and politics of the Far East. (The only areas I studied at Kent State were Europe and Latin America.) I struggled with the Sino-Soviet Pact, the causes of the war with Japan. Too soon, the bell announced that our time was up. It would be six months before they let us know whether or not we passed that "God-awful" exam.

In June 1945, I returned to Kent State for Commencement. I was the first woman at Kent to graduate with a B.S. degree in Business Administration. With a 3.0 average, straight "A"s in all the business and economics courses, I was graduated magna cum laude. Ed Curry, Sr., who would hardly speak to me during the four years I attended KSU, was in the audience to applaud the loudest. (The Goodyear plant had been on strike that spring, but the President ordered the Navy to take over and my father went back to work.) Some 20 years later, after my success in the field of business, I was invited to Smith College to receive an *honorary* degree—but that's another story.

After Commencement, I returned to Washington. On August 7, 1945, the war in the Pacific ended, a few days after President Harry S Truman made the decision to drop the first atomic bombs on Hiroshima and Nagasaki. I went to Mass to pray for a lasting peace. Then, with three friends from the office, I boarded the Pennsylvania Railroad for New York, the *only* place to be on V-J Day. Flags were flying over Times Square, a solid mass of humanity shouting and carousing, total strangers grabbing anyone in sight for a kiss. The four of us were "man-less, drink-less, but hilarious" on that historic occasion. The next morning I went to Point Lookout to collapse and get some much-needed R & R with "Aunt Bern" Sweeney.

Back in Washington, I found that long-awaited government-franked envelope in my mail box with the results of the Foreign Service exam. The routine bureaucratic forms then had no space for scores, only Pass or Fail. Miraculously, I passed. I waited impatiently for news of my overseas assignment. Early dreams of Paris or London were shattered when my first posting arrived. It was to Saudi Arabia, a country where native women were then (and still are) heavily veiled, and foreign women who dared to show their faces on the streets were often spit upon. I was more concerned about the sanitary conditions. Dysentary, pneumonia, and tuberculosis threatened one's health, not to mention what the heat and humidity could do to it. With some misgivings, I turned that first assignment down. Then, as in so many other difficult situations of my life, my good luck held out. Someone in the upper echelon decided that Saudi Arabia was not a compatible post for a young, single woman. Perhaps because of my knowledge of German, I was reassigned to Munich, the city in Bavaria known for good music and Oktoberfest.

It would be some time before they could find a replacement for me in the office. I had Thanksgiving dinner with the Dodds, a 15-pound turkey with all the trimmings, and washed the dishes as usual—but this time with a lump in my throat. I realized how much I would miss this wonderful family that had given me shelter when I first came to Washington.

I wanted to be closer to the office that last winter. The only way I would be able to afford an apartment was to share with two other girls. We finally found what we were looking for at 2816 Connecticut, at that time the "Park Avenue" of Washington. The rent was high at that address, even for a small one-bedroom (with twin beds and a cot), but we liked the open fireplace and bookcases. It was very conveniently located two blocks from the Shoreham Hotel, seven minutes from downtown, and ten steps from the bus stop. One room-mate was a softspoken Irish lass from Oberlin College in Ohio. The other, Stella Ferrara, was a Phi Beta Kappa from the University of Alabama. Stella had studied at the University of Mexico and spoke fluent Spanish, *muy simpático*. We discovered that we could eat well by contributing $6 a piece to the "kitty" every two weeks, with a diet heavy in meat loaf and chicken a la king. I bragged to my mother that I had become a marvelous cook. (My adult children still groan when I tell them about the Clark Bar and ice-water parties with which we entertained our friends.)

We were almost settled by the time I took the train home for Christmas. My parents were still waiting for my brother to return. Friends in Akron were marrying their old school loves—everyone but Peggy. With Foreign Service experience, I was sure I would have no trouble in finding an import-export job in Akron after I returned; then I would marry, have children, and become a typical American housewife.

I still considered Webb Colfield a possibility. For New Year's Eve, I took the B&O railroad to Chicago to meet him. We had a great time, but it didn't settle anything. I wrote afterwards to my parents that it was an unnecessary expense of time and energy.

Shortly after I returned to Washington, my brother Ed walked into the office one morning, unannounced. What a reunion! We talked non-stop through an afternoon of sightseeing and dinner at my apartment. He was on his way to New York, excited that he had been accepted at Columbia University Graduate School.

After Ed settled in New York, I visited him often. In the cafeteria line one day I bumped into Dan Wargowsky, the vice president of the East High student council who succeeded me. He was now at Columbia graduate school. Small world! Ed Sweeney and my friend Eleanor Bowman formed a foursome with Ed, Jr. and me on weekends in Forest Hills. Another old friend, Harry Eich, very handsome in his uniform and just returned from overseas, took me dancing at Roseland. I soon realized Harry was good only for fun and games, not for the long haul.

In January, I passed the Foreign Service physical. It was now official that I would be assigned to Munich, but I was still waiting for a replacement to take over my job. In the meantime, I kept busy with activities in the Department. It pleased me to be among the chosen few when the new Secretary of State, James F. Byrnes, looking just like "the guy up the street,"

The Curry Family 1945: Catherine, Ed Jr., Julia, and Ed Sr.

Peggy Curry Goes To Washington

talked to fourteen of the junior officers in the Diplomatic
Reception Rooms.

Anne Gibbons, just back from Lima, Peru, invited me to
a formal dinner at her apartment (her father was a former
Under Secretary of the Treasury). I also signed up to represent
my division on the recreation program, assisting at the
Department dance at the old Wardman-Park Hotel (now the
Sheraton). My date for the evening was Major William
Freedman of the First (African) Division, covered with decorations and just back from three years overseas during the worst
fighting in Sicily and Normandy.

Another beau had more serious intentions. Bill Cobb, a
Foreign Service officer, took me dancing at the Shoreham the
night that he proposed and offered the "family diamond."
He was leaving soon for an assignment in Havana, Cuba, and
wanted me to come along as his wife. He was a wonderful guy,
but I didn't love him, so I turned him down. His family hoped
I would change my mind. I was "his girl" at a lovely farewell
party at the Westchester apartments hosted by his uncle,
a Federal judge. I was still dating Ed Clark, a Princeton man
from Philadelphia, who invited me to a candlelight dinner
with uniformed maid to serve, demitasses after in the library,
at his uncle's impressive home. Ed was my escort to a formal
dance at the Willard Hotel for State Department and
American Foreign Service personnel hosted by Virginia
Berrier, a State Department friend, whose father was a Vice
President of AT&T. Ed and I also attended a beautiful wedding reception of another Foreign Service chum. A four-star
general was the father of the groom, and there was more
Army brass there than I could count. Marriage appeared to
be contagious in post-World War II Washington.
Everybody was doing it.

Another very special friend I liked to go dancing with was
Crosby Wells, who lost a leg on the battlefield. We went to the

Mayflower ballroom for his first dance since he was hit, and the Carlton soon thereafter. I hoped to convince him he was still a good dancer and hadn't lost his way with women. Crosby also invited me to dinner at the home of a well-to-do friend on the banks of the Potomac in Maryland. What fun we had, riding back to Washington in his Buick convertible with the top down, hair flying in the breeze. I shall never forget those good times. I am grateful that God blessed me with enthusiasm. I really got a kick out of life, and I still do.

In March, I started to break in my replacement, then went home to Akron for a last visit before Munich. I had my choice of sailing May 1 on the S.S. *Brazil*, or May 4, on another luxury liner converted during the war to a Liberty Ship. There was no reason to delay. I asked my parents to come to Washington at the end of April to see me off. They stayed at the old Brighton Hotel on California Street for a few days, then all of us took the train to New York to visit Ed before I boarded the *Brazil*.

I can only imagine my mother's feelings on the pier in New York harbor, waving goodbye to her only daughter departing for war-ravaged Europe. (She had suffered silently when my brother Ed joined the Air Force and flew the Hump in the Burma/India theater of operations.) For my part, the excitement over seeing new places I had only read about outweighed the qualms I felt in the pit of my stomach.

Peggy Curry with John Montgomery in Munich where
they first met.

CHAPTER TWO

From Preston Avenue To Prinzregentenstrasse

THE S.S. BRAZIL was crowded with foreign nationals returning to their homelands. Among the other passengers were a few adventuresome American tourists who wanted to see what was left of Europe, and government personnel like myself, enroute to their first overseas posts. My address for the next two years would be: American Consulate General, APO 407-A, c/o Postmaster, New York.

My friend Dot Case, who had been serving with the Red Cross overseas for the past six months, met me at the port of Calais. A friend of hers, a young lieutenant, offered to drive me to Paris in his Army jeep. At that time, Foreign Service personnel were billeted at the Crillon, the elegant four-star hotel near the American Embassy. After the War it was a bit worse for the wear, but still luxury-plus to a young woman from Middle America.

I arrived in the City of Light in the spring of 1946, just in time to celebrate the anniversary of the Liberation. I was lucky to be there on this historic occasion, something to write home about. From dawn to dark, Parisians filled the streets, celebrating and singing the *Marseillaise*, showing their gratitude to all American soldiers and civilians within reach with hugs and kisses on both cheeks. For the first time in many years, the lights came on again at sunset, a stirring sight.

The next day, I boarded the overnight train to Munich. The beautiful tree-lined Prinzregentenstrasse, a street of fine 19th-century buildings, had been devastated by the Allied bombing. Photos in American newspapers had revealed some of the war damage, but I was unprepared for the total destruction I saw with my own eyes. Daily raids had turned Munich into a pile of rubble. Bombed-out buildings on every street were constant reminders, the scraggly trees were stunted and charred. The U.S. Army requisitioned the few buildings still intact, including the one that housed the American Consulate and the largest transmitter of the "Voice of America" in Europe. An old-fashioned trolley car that ran the length of the Ludwigstrasse, the main street, was our only means of transportation save for Army staff cars and jeeps.

I was assigned to an apartment on the top floor of an impressive building—Prinzregentenstrasse, 21—far different from the modest home of the Currys on Preston Avenue in Akron. From the balcony I had a clear view of the vast open spaces of the English Garden where horse-drawn carriages were still for hire. It was sad to see only remnants of the pre-war landscaping.

Janie Heether, a young woman of about my age from Florida, was my apartment-mate. We became close friends. As small-town Americans, we never lost our amazement at the high exchange-rate of the dollar, the Polish maid who kept our apartment spotless, the unlimited privileges at the Officers' Club. Since much of the local economy was still based on barter, we could also use American cigarettes as money. Each U.S. staff member was allowed a carton a week at the PX, and each carton was worth $20. A non-smoker, I was able to sell my share and gain extra dollars to contribute to the Catholic orphanage.

My first day on the job I reported to Consul General Samuel Wood. Wood came to Munich from Geneva, where he held the important post of wartime Ambassador to Switzerland. His wife, Wilhelmina Busch, a daughter of the well-known Anheuser-Busch family of St. Louis, Missouri, was a gracious woman who made me feel very much at home as part of the consular "family."

One of my first friends at the consulate was Dorothy Jester, Sam Wood's secretary. She was about 40, fluent in English, and very knowledgeable about the U.S. Before the war, she had been secretary to the head of the Ford Motor Company in Berlin. She spent the war years in the heavily-bombed section of that city, and told me about many close calls. I realized how fortunate my family was to live in Mid-America, where our only direct involvement with the war was recycling scrap paper and tin cans.

In July I phoned my parents in Akron on their 26th wedding anniversary, and they reported my activities to the *Beacon-Journal*. As administrative assistant in the personnel department, I was reviewing applications of local Münchens for work in the Consulate.

One of the women I befriended was Erne Brucher, a Roumanian, who later visited me in the States and became a U.S. citizen in 1955. Erne complained that the food wasn't as good in the cafeteria where the locals ate as it was in the Army mess. I volunteered to have lunch with her to prove that she was wrong. When we walked into the dining room, the smell of sauerkraut and over-cooked sausage was so overpowering I almost fainted! After that experience, I organized a campaign to serve the same G.I. food we ate to the local employees in their cafeteria.

Soon after I arrived in Munich, I noticed there were very few recreational facilities for young German women. With so many G.I.s in the area and nowhere to go for wholesome entertainment, the situation might soon get out of hand. It was my idea to organize a place like the YWCA, where young women 16 to 20 could get together after hours. Kenneth MacCormac, the Public Affairs Officer, agreed to help me out. Mac requisitioned an ex-Wehrmacht barracks on the outskirts and had it moved to a central location. The City of Munich donated the land. We put G.I. carpenters to work and hired an old German couple to help maintain the building. The local Board of Education donated a piano. Several civilians turned up with radios and a record player. Our work together at Friendship House was the beginning of a lifelong friendship with "Mac." What started as a romantic attachment—more on his part than mine—endured through the best of times and the worst of times, through my two marriages, and ended only with Mac's death in his eighties. Until then, he was always there when I needed him, and I miss him now.

Some 40 German girls brought together by the Bavarian Welfare Agency, "Jugendsamt," attended the first planning session for Friendship House. From this group, we put together an executive committee of six German and six American women. It was a success from the beginning. Frau Ihmig, who taught German classes to Embassy personnel, started a series of bi-lingual training courses in accounting to help the girls get good jobs. Some took sewing and music lessons. A German social worker, Dr. Stautner, came to counsel girls from war-disrupted homes, including the D.P.s (Displaced Persons) from a nearby camp. There was a day-care facility for younger children, many of whose fathers were still Russian prisoners-of-war. G.I.s donated Army sports equipment. American volunteers, Army wives and members of the consulate, stocked the library and served on alternating shifts. We initiated discussion groups to improve the girls' language skills—and ours.

One of the biggest problems was to get the German girls to think and act for themselves. Their men had led them to believe they were fit only for "*kinder, kirche,* and *kuchen.*" We tried to teach them something about our American customs. They especially enjoyed the Virginia Reel and other folk dances. In the beginning, Friendship House was intended for the girls' recreation only—G.I.s were *verboten* (forbidden). But when the G.I.s heard about the good times they were missing, they wanted to come to the folk dances. As a natural consequence, several of the girls met and married American soldiers and followed them to the U.S.

With my job and other activities in Munich, there wasn't much time for travel. When we went on leave that winter, my apartment-mate from sunny Florida talked me into a weekend in the Alpine ski resort of St. Moritz. Mac MacCormac and some of his buddies went with us. None of us had skied before, so we spent as much time *in* the snow as on top of it. In those days, skis were long, skinny wooden slats that had to be waxed after every use. One measured the length of the skis by one's height, plus an arm's-reach over the head. For tall people, this was a disaster; we had twice as far to fall! In spite of which, we had a good time horsing around on the slopes during the daytime, drinking German mulled wine and warming ourselves in front of the fire at night.

I was too busy to be homesick. There were parties every weekend at the Officers' Club. The circus with amazing juggling and acrobatic acts came from Eastern Europe. In spring, there was "Fasching," or Carnival, to mark the beginning of Lent, with parades and dancing and masquerading in costume. (Someone told me that medieval monks mastered the art of brewing to sustain them during the fasting period!) In summer, I spent many sunny days in the English Garden across the street.

Nearby on the Prinzregentenstrasse was the Haus der Kunst, a vast building from the Nazi era, where Army personnel and those of us who worked at the Consulate took most of our meals. (We were not supposed to eat out in local restaurants; it would deprive Germans of scarce food.) On the wide porch-like annex in back, exhibitions of avant-garde art were held. The Haus was open till all hours, a place to get together with one's friends, with entertainment and music for dancing after dinner every night.

With 90 men to every woman, I was having the best time of my life, with no thoughts of marriage. Until one evening Mac MacCormac introduced me to a tall, handsome tank officer from the 2nd Constabulary Brigade. He had been in the worst fighting of the Battle of the Bulge with General George Patton, had looked death in the face, both in battle and in liberating one of the ugliest of the German concentration camps.

I won't say it was love at first sight, but there was instant attraction. As the days went by, I discovered that John Montgomery, unlike many American officers, was not just counting time until he completed his Army service and could return home. He was interested in the world around him, studying the German language, visiting in German homes. He was a serious man, a thoughtful man. We liked the same people, enjoyed the same activities.

One of our mutual enthusiasms was skiing. Both novices, we soon enrolled in a ski school and graduated to the more difficult slopes at St. Moritz (affordable because of the favorable exchange rate of the dollar). Sometimes we would chaperone groups of German girls from Friendship House at the nearby ski areas.

Our first Christmas together was very special. With a light dusting of snow, the war-bombed buildings of Munich looked like gingerbread houses. The *Tannenbaum* (Christmas tree) plays an important role in German Christmases, and treasured decorations came out of wartime hiding. G.I.s went out of their way to see that no child was hungry.

On the Friday before Christmas, the Mayor of Munich invited us to a Christmas party for some 200 children of the war-torn city, including the refugee children, to be held in the Council Hall of the Rathaus. A chorus of pupils from the Municipal Kindergarten Seminary sang "Ihr Kinderlein kommet" (Come ye children), and the Mayor, Dr. Scharnagl, spoke a few words. We were all amused and touched by "Münchner Kindlwiegn" (Munich Rocking the Cradle), a charming Christmas play performed by a children's group, the "Singkreis Nord." There were not many dry eyes in the audience when we finished off the evening, singing carols together and distributing gifts to the needy children.

John and I celebrated Christmas Eve together at the Officers' Club, decorated with holly and pine branches. After the feast of the Christmas goose with chestnut stuffing and many toasts, we lingered around the fire. Some of us trooped off to the Cathedral for midnight Mass. I shall never forget those strong male voices booming out "Adeste Fideles," nor their rendering "Stille Nacht, Heilige Nacht" on that very special night. After mass, we went back to the apartment for breakfast.

When the Hungarian Opera came to Munich in April 1947, John got tickets and asked if he might bring some of the members of the cast to my apartment afterwards for a party. That is when I met Sari Barbas, the beautiful coloratura soprano who sang the role of "Queen of the Night" in Mozart's *Magic Flute*. Sari fled Budapest in a horse-drawn wagon before the advancing Russian Army. At that time she did not know the meaning of the English word, "refugee," but she learned it in a hurry. She grabbed the satin sheets from her bed and fled.

They covered the straw pallet in the back of the wagon where she and her mother and sister-in-law huddled for the next 29 days. When they finally came to the village of Pasau, they knocked on the door of the priest, who took them in. They were still hiding from the Russians until that happy day when the Americans came.

Three officers of the 83rd Armored Division arrived at the priest's house bearing gifts, the first coffee anyone had seen since the beginning of the war and a rare chicken. The chicken was old and stringy, but it was the best meal they had had in a very long time. Sari's mother drank so much coffee she almost had heart palpitations! After dinner, Sari played the priest's harmonium and everyone sang old familiar songs like "Make Believe" and "Let Me Love You Tonight."

One of the tank officers at the priest's house that evening was John Montgomery. He was attracted to that beautiful girl with the coloratura soprano voice and had a close, but stormy relationship with her before he met Peg Curry from Ohio. John wrote to me later that he couldn't understand "the strange state I allowed myself to get into over her...now it seems amazing that I could have been so blind." (After meeting Sari, I could certainly understand the attraction!) She has continued to be my lifelong friend, and visited me most recently in Washington during the Christmas holidays in 1993.

II

As a U.S. Embassy employee, I was permitted to import a small Ford for use during my tour of duty in Germany. John and I were eager to test it out. The summer of 1947, we took our leave together to see another part of Europe, the Scandinavian countries. This may have been the beginning of my lifelong love of travel. The first night after Munich, we drove to Darmstadt, just south of Frankfurt, a town in the line of battle after the crossing of the Rhine—as the Germans say, *sehr zerstort* (ravaged). Early the next morning, we headed for Hamburg, the so-called "Venice of the North," through the English zone, from Frankfurt via Kassel to Hanover. Friends from the Consulate there arranged for us to stay at a luxurious hotel facing the big alster (lake). Despite visible ruins, the hotel had something of its pre-war air of luxury, the best the British had to offer in Germany. Some of our Consulate friends entertained us at the Officer's Country Club, a dignified old estate the Brits had requisitioned.

Hamburg was a gay and cosmopolitan city before the British took their revenge for the bombing of London. When we saw it, one section was referred to as the "dead city"; for blocks and blocks there was not one single building left standing, even the bricks were pulverized.

We had to go to the U.S. Consulate to get a permit to exit the American zone before leaving Hamburg. Early the next morning we headed north through Schleswig-Holstein to the Danish border, driving through acres and acres of beautiful farmland with cows grazing peacefully. The roads were well laid out and the Ford was a big improvement over the Army jeeps, so we zipped right along. By supper time we arrived in Fredicia and enjoyed our first restaurant meal: to our surprise, American-style chicken fried in butter, fresh green salad, new potatoes and strawberry shortcake to remind us of home— plus that wonderful Danish coffee. That dinner was a rare treat, after months of the Army mess.

Then we pushed on to the Isle of Fyn, where we had a good night's sleep and rose early to take the ferry to the main island of Denmark. Just after noon, we were enjoying the beauties of Copenhagen. We dressed and went dancing that evening at an exclusive club, untouched by the war. During the seven-course dinner, we listened to the strains of Strauss and Schubert. Shortly after 9 o'clock, the concert orchestra was replaced by a swing band. Imagine my surprise when those handsome

Danes stood up and burst forth with a popular song of the time, "Open the door, Richard"! (Another example of the American culture being felt around the world.)

For the next two days we became acquainted with the Danes and their lovely capital. In Copenhagen, we visited palaces, watched the Changing of the Guard at the King's home, surveyed old buildings and gazed at picture galleries. The second night, we went to a concert by members of the Milan Opera Company. The third evening, we ferried from Copenhagen to Malmo in Sweden, where we parked the Ford and took a luxurious European sleeping car.

We awoke at 9 A.M. in Stockholm and found it clean and orderly beyond imagination. The people seemed so wealthy compared to the rest of the Europeans, but the city lacked the friendly air that made Copenhagen so much fun. Some of our British friends recommended the Hotel Saltsjobaden, a luxurious old palace some twenty miles up the Archipelago. After a few days in that exalted atmosphere, I almost acquired an Oxford accent!

Most of the time in Stockholm was spent getting acquainted with the cooperative system we had heard so much about. We went through factories and housing developments, childrens' playgrounds and other social projects that represented the Swedish government's aim to make life better for all its citizens. There seemed to be no poverty, and the food was abundant and more tasty than any place in Europe at that time. We could not overlook the fact that the Swedes suffered comparatively little from the war, in fact they seemed to have profited from it. They had just made a trade treaty with Russia, their great neighbor to the East, that involved exporting a large percentage of their production in return for a promise to pay in 25 years—a post-war attempt of the Swedes to straddle the political fence again.

On Sunday morning, we caught the Dutch airline to Oslo. On a clear day, flying over the lake region, Norway looked like a "fairyland" below. We were greeted by one of the Vice Consuls formerly stationed in Munich. But Oslo was disappointing, not at all what I expected. With only 300,000 people, it could easily have been mistaken for any small town in Wisconsin or Minnesota. It was hit very hard by the war. Though the Norwegians are strong and courageous, the people—and the buildings—showed the strain of the German occupation. For some seven years they lived on fish and potatoes. We were invited to eat in the officers' mess because the local economy was so poor. To visitors, the lobster and shrimp featured on every menu was a rare treat, but I can imagine one would become tired of fish after so many years!

At Malmo we picked up the Ford again. The drive crossing the strait back to Denmark was about the loveliest part of the trip, and arriving back in Copenhagen seemed like coming home. We decided there were enough days of leave-time remaining to travel to the Lowland countries. We stayed at Fredicia again, and the next morning motored towards the German border. I was an inexperienced navigator, so we ended up 240 kilometers out of our way. Instead of crossing into Germany, we were gazing out on the North Sea. The view was so beautiful, I didn't mind, but I could tell John, the driver, was not quite so happy.

We reached the German border about noon, and went back to Hamburg enroute Bremen, refueled and stopped for dinner. Then we drove on to Holland and spent the night at a typical little Dutch inn in the town of Hengelo. We drank beer and talked pidgin German and pidgin English until the wee hours.

The Dutch impressed me as having survived the war better than expected, though they suffered the greatest economic setbacks. Their accounts of the Occupation were grim tales (about which most of us in America have now become familiar). One reflection of national pride and resistance was their refusal to speak German to the occupying army, though most of them were fluent in that language. They were quick to point out that there was a great difference between individual soldiers and the Nazi government. For instance, the occupying forces had been, in most cases, kind to the Dutch children.

Arnhem, our next stop, almost completely destroyed by bombs, had been the scene of seven months of fighting. We passed the Queen's summer residence at Apeldoorn and drove down narrow little roads past lovely villages to Amsterdam. Its canals, narrow streets and old buildings seemed to be bent by the ages.

We were off the next morning to the Isle of Mark, still untouched by progress. It was a great contrast to Volendam, which—even so soon after the War—was too commercialized and lacked charm. (The Dutch soon caught on to the idea that there was money to be made posing for photos in their wooden shoes!) Then we drove north to the great dike which closes off the Zuider Zee from the North Sea, an interesting engineering phenomenon. (We saw it before the Dutch reclaimed some half-million acres of farmland from the Zuider Zee.)

In The Hague, we visited the Palace of Justice, the Queen's winter residence, the House of Parliament and other government buildings, then drove on to Rotterdam. Not much was left of the great seaport. Immense blocks of the former business district were destroyed in 1941 by German bombs. That evening we enjoyed a cabaret with lots of atmosphere in Heerlen, a small town near the German border.

Sunday morning we rose early and re-entered Germany just west of Aachen. Of the whole trip, the drive from Aachen to Frankfurt left the greatest impression, because of the indescribable war damage. In Julich, for example, *nothing* remained of what must have been a lovely little German town, similar to many in Holland. The only thing left standing in the midst of

Traveling was a common enjoyment which Julia and John shared.

the ruins was the beautiful cathedral in Cologne.

From Cologne to Frankfurt I was reminded of the old melody about castles on the Rhine. The ruins of the Romans and the more recent medieval castles of the robber barons are both colorful parts of German history. Many small Swiss and Norwegian vessels plied the Rhine that summer, though German trade was at a standstill. We arrived in Frankfurt in time for dinner, then hurried down the Autobahn to Munich, ending two weeks of sightseeing in postwar Europe.

I jotted in my travel letters and diary that I had looked forward to seeing these places in Europe since childhood. For instance, Venice is one of the most romantic cities in the world and when I finally got there, it seemed almost like living a dream. In those days the exchange rate was so favorable we could afford to stay at the Gritti Palace Hotel on the Grand Canal, with gondolas gliding by underneath our window. We sampled the famous peach drink at Harry's American Bar, and explored the twisty, cobblestoned streets around the Bridge of Sighs. I returned later in life whenever I could find the time. The world is a very small place, and I have always wondered how wars could start, when people everywhere are so much alike.

From Preston Avenue To Prinzregentenstrasse

John and I got along very well throughout these trips. I remember only two tiffs, one in Amsterdam and another at the magnificent hotel in Saltsjoban. (I can't recall the cause in Holland. Perhaps in the latter case it was my "British" accent?) Travel is a difficult test, and we knew that our love was good for the "long haul."

Soon after we returned to Munich, my brother Ed, just out of the Air Force, arrived with a friend from Ohio, Alan Burrell. The boys stayed with me, and John and I took them sightseeing around the city. I was happy that John could meet another member of the Curry family. After they left Munich, the boys decided to live it up in Paris, and from there went on to Switzerland.

My roommate, Janie Heether, Mac MacCormac and I drove over to pick them up the first week in August. On the way back to Munich we stayed for the first five days in the lovely resort town of Garmisch-Partenkirchen with its colorful chalets surrounded by mountains. (Garmisch has since become a favorite place for our family, and all of my children have visited there.)

The next weekend we drove over to Berchtesgaden, Adolf Hitler's summer home, a two-story chalet with a very large picture window overlooking the Bavarian Alps. We were surprised to find the "Eagle's Nest" so sparsely furnished, with no remnants of the mighty Führer who changed the course of history and ruined so many lives. We stayed in a hotel in the U.S. Army recreation area near Lake Eibsee, where we hiked, enjoyed the hearty American food, and bathed in the sun before heading back to Munich.

❧ III

A year later, in March 1948, Sari Barbas returned to Munich. When she asked, "What's new?" I replied, "John Montgomery and I are going to be married."

Sari was not surprised. For some time, she had suspected that our relationship was deepening. She had already formed an attachment with someone else, and had come to ask my advice.

John and I, too, had a few problems, but I felt sure we could work them out. The Catholic faith was, and still is, a very important part of my life, on which my values are based. John would not—and could not, because of a previous marriage—be married in the Church. But he and my mother agreed on the subject of religion. "We are all good Christians: that's the important thing."

Our good friend Mac, who introduced us, seemed thrilled when he heard the news of the Montgomery-Curry partnership. He said he always thought we were perfect for each other. He admired and liked John and expected great things of him.

Having made the decision to marry, I went to Sam Wood to tell him about our future plans. He wished me happiness, said that John was a very fine man, but added that he would hate to lose me—I was the most competent young woman he had ever had in his department! Though I appreciated such praise, it did not influence my decision to marry. But no-one had told me when I joined the Foreign Service that when a woman married, she was automatically fired from her job. With my good record, it never occurred to me that I would have to choose between the Service and a husband. I planned to continue with my work, at least as long as John was stationed in Munich.

In October, John got his orders to return home and head the National Guard unit in Washington State. I agreed to stay on until spring to tie up the loose ends of my Foreign Service job and my work at Friendship House. Like so many women of that era, I disliked giving up my own meaningful work, but decided that marriage was more important.

It was lonely without John, but I managed to fill my time. In a sample week, I played bridge with several of John's friends and Mac, the Public Affairs Officer, on Tuesday; Wednesday, it was Friendship House 'til 8:30, then a Polish liaison officer, a buddy of John's, came to call. Thursday, Mac took me to the premiere of one of the new German films and a press party. I was never so pursued by men before I became engaged! I could have had a date every night, but my heart was still with that Army major in Washington State.

We kept in touch almost daily with letters. Immediately after landing in New York, John had his wallet stolen, an eye-opener to the perils of life in the good ol' USA. After so many years overseas, he was already discontent and disillusioned with the contemporary American way of life. "I find myself partly a foreigner with yearnings for Europe, and a discerning and critical eye which sees much in America that can be civilized and softened," he wrote. He was determined to return to Germany, where we had been so happy together.

Enroute to Seattle, John detoured to Washington, D.C., to take the Foreign Service exam at the State Department—"with all my hopes tied up in it"—and stopped off in Akron to meet my parents. Then followed a monotonous cross-country drive through Indiana, Illinois, Nebraska, Wyoming, and Idaho, to Spokane, Washington, where he visited his old friend, Welly Bingham.

When he arrived in Seattle, he was bothered by what he presumed was a "nervous stomach." Doctors at the nearby Washington State Army hospital checked him in for tests. They diagnosed a serious ulcer condition, and ordered six-to-eight weeks of bed rest, a diet of half milk/half cream and soft-boiled egg once a day—and *not to worry*. How could my high-strung hero stop worrying, with what he considered a meaningless job, an uncertain future, and his popular fiancee 6,000 miles away?

Risks & Rewards

The final blow came when the results of the Foreign Service exam were posted on December 11, just before Christmas. When John got the bad news, he wrote: "They passed me up, perhaps for good." He almost forgot to mention the *good* news: he made a passing grade in all but the foreign language section. (John spoke fluent German, but had not studied the grammar.) There would be another opportunity to take the exam in Seattle in March.

I could tell from John's letters that he was deeply disappointed and depressed about our future. In February, he was released from the hospital. "The doctor said my condition should continue to improve, and I should have no further trouble," he wrote. "I'm not supposed to worry or to be under nervous tension. Of course, I *always* worry…I feel insecure in my job…and our whole future depends on it."

As instructor and advisor to the battalion, John had endless routine forms to fill out, a great deal of bureaucratic administrative work which he found frustrating. He was also trying to equip and buy furniture for our first home: "I never realized what starting a house from scratch meant," he wrote. Was it his health, the hard physical labor of getting the house ready, the job, or a combination of the three that caused his deepening depression? He wrote to "dearest Peggy" on one of those "dark, gray melancholy days, with wet slushy snow falling and dark gray gloom hanging everywhere." He was also worrying about world problems over which he had no control. (He predicted, rightly, future conflicts with the Soviet Union.)

"1948 has been a wretched year for me, nothing seems to go right," he announced in a typical letter. "The one obsession of my life is a fear of failure. I felt honor bound to make this particular point clear to you…it, and no other, was the reason the marriage between Martha [John's first wife] and me failed. She never knew how upset I became about insecurity of the future…I have nothing to offer you except my pessimism and despair…it's all a dull routine, and I don't know what would be the outlet for all that endless energy and creativeness of yours." With true insight, he added: "We seem capable of solving our problems when we are together, apart [I am] lonesome and adrift."

"Dear John (I replied in my next letter): …despite your pessimism, I feel sure that as soon as we are together, everything will be wonderful. Of course, we'll have problems, but life would be too awfully dull if we didn't, and as for your particular problems, I believe them to be very *good* signs. Once you become a bit more philosophical, I'm sure you'll agree with me. I have no reservations about our marriage. I think we can be completely happy in Pakistan or Prague [with the Foreign Service]—or Centralia. I am most concerned about the state of affairs of the world, too…I share your frustration…You contribute so much to society in your own way, but it is never quite enough for your own satisfaction, and that, darling, is one of the biggest reasons for my loving you so much… but we must keep our balance and work very hard." I've always been a cockeyed optimist, and this situation was no exception. I urged John to concentrate on German grammar and passing the Foreign Service exam. It wouldn't be long until spring, then I would be there to cheer him up.

My family was still hoping that John would take time off to come to Ohio for an Easter wedding. My father wasn't well enough to make the trip West, and it would mean so much to Mother to have the ceremony at home. I promised John "a minimum of fuss."

My future mother-in-law Helen Montgomery wrote, urging me to hurry West, that my coming would be so good for her son. "Really, my dear, I think he has some secret fear that you won't ever get here." John had put in a fine vegetable garden on the hill behind the house, she reported; there would be peas and corn, lettuce and tomatoes, melons and squash—

and trout in our brook! Our neighbors were nice people and Helen was sure I would like them, but "I think John worries that it will be dull for you, you've had such an exciting career," she added. "I'm sure you'll love it this summer…the fruit trees will be in blossom when you get here."

Helen had consulted our astrological charts, and discovered they were compatible. (I have the same ascendant as Woodrow Wilson and Napoleon!) The stars also revealed my rare talent for organization. "You are incapable of being anything but completely honest," she wrote, "you two are going to be a glorious success together."

In February, with some regret, I handed Sam Wood my resignation. Those last days in Munich were busy ones, with the dressmaker (lovely white satin gown, blue tweed suit), packing, callers, and commissary. The Foreign Service staff gave a going-away cocktail party for me. Some 80 or 100 people came. I didn't realize I had so many friends in Munich.

Saying goodbye to my German friends was more difficult. The Alien employees gave a farewell tea for me, and it seemed so final, really touching. It was not like any other goodbyes I've ever said. I had kept my departure as quiet as possible to prevent undue fuss, but everyone found out somehow. The little girls at Friendship House all wept and just wouldn't stop, and I wept too. I collected enough Bavarian mementos from them to furnish a *schloss*!

My good friend Mac, the PAO, insisted on driving me to Paris to catch the boat-train. I was so tired after the farewells that I slept in the car all the way to Stuttgart, before stopping in Frankfurt for the night. On Valentine's Day, we arrived in Paris and booked into the Hotel Crillon on the historic Place de la Concorde. I wrote to John that in spite of Mac's good intentions: "[He] couldn't quite keep up *our* pace of museums, castles, churches and art galleries, but he certainly tried." We saw the Mona Lisa, the Venus de Milo, and the Winged

Victory, but it would have taken another three months to see *all* of the Louvre. We had cocktails the last night at the Ritz, dinner at Maxim's, and liqueurs at the very fashionable George V (pronounced `sank'). I picked up some new records for our collection in my last minutes of shopping, thinking of *you* all the time." (The above itinerary was a possible dream in the days when the dollar was king.) I was sorry that John couldn't have been with me to enjoy Paris, but I was sure we'd do it together some day.

I was booked for a crossing on the S.S. *America*, one of the luxury ships of the United States Line. Mac escorted me to the boat train with two ORCHIDS as a farewell gift—always the sophisticated man-about-town—when he said goodbye. I was deeply grateful, and sorry I couldn't reciprocate the affection and attention he showered on me. In spite of this royal treatment, I felt sure in my heart that I had made the right decision. Mac would always be a good friend, but I was *in love*—with John.

The *America* lived up to all expectations for glamour and excitement. This floating hotel was almost beyond belief to the young American girl I was, plain Peg Curry. I wrote to John that the double room with private bath I shared with my State Department friend made the Gritti Palace Hotel appear second rate. With a swimming pool and gym, an excellent library, movies, bars, and night clubs, we never lacked for entertainment. I was so busy playing deck tennis, swimming, promenading and dancing that there was little time for sleep. We had only five days at sea to enjoy the trip; I wished it would last forever. My typical schedule was breakfast in bed at ten, a swim and exercise in the gym until one, then lunch, followed by 30 turns around the promenade deck and lifeboat drill.

There were lots of attractive people aboard, some of whom showered me with more attention than I thought I deserved. Among the fellow passengers were Lawrence Armour, Jr., heir to the Armour meat-packing fortune, and Victor Vargas Boussert, an Argentinian whose father owned the Suchard Chocolate Company. I found the former dull and a bit stuffy (in spite of any financial considerations!). The latter was very intelligent and had recently published an article in *Harper's* monthly magazine, "Why the Argentinians Voted for Peron." (Victor was only 5'8", shorter than I am in my stocking feet.)

After a few days at sea, I volunteered for a job with a State Department mission investigating the steel situation in Europe. It was headed by a bright young ex-Professor of Economics from Amherst College very much in need of someone to type and edit his report. It proved fascinating, but when the Professor offered me a permanent job as administrative assistant, I replied, "No, thanks. I'm off to a much more exciting future, with an MRS. degree!" The chance encounters on the boat only convinced me that John, no other, was Mr. Right for me.

The last day at sea, I awoke at seven and felt the boat "rocking and rolling." I remembered the Old Wives' advice to prevent sea-sickness: eat something to fill an empty stomach. I hurried to the dining room, only to have a tremendous wave tip the table and spill coffee and orange juice on my lap! I crawled back to my cabin and slept until noon, when I began to feel much better.

Janie Heether, my Munich roommate, had been sent back to the States on medical leave. She had now recovered and was on the dock to meet me in New York. We booked into the Hotel Biltmore for three days, then drove down to D.C., where I was on temporary assignment to the State Department. Jane and I were happy to be roommates again. I moved into her spacious apartment at 2201 Massachusetts Avenue near Dupont Circle.

I was worried about John, impatient to finish my job and to head West. The day finally came when I handed in my papers

and collected my "retirement" pay nest egg of $3,000. Jane and
I went home for the first visit to Preston Avenue since I left
for Europe.

My parents were disappointed not to have the wedding of
their only daughter in Akron. We had taken into consideration
John's previous marriage, his precarious ulcer, and the religious
factor, and decided on a simple civil ceremony at our new
home in Washington State. The Currys graciously settled for a
large "open house" and engagement party for our many rela-
tives and friends. Every time we walked down the street, one
of my childhood chums would stop to talk and catch up with
the news of the past several years. My brother Ed was also
home for a visit, and with Jane as our houseguest and my
approaching marriage, there was a constant round of parties. I
was an exhausted bride by the time Mother and I boarded the
"City of Portland" on the first lap of our journey to the Far
West via Chicago, and my new life as Mrs. John Montgomery.

Julia Curry Montgomery with new husband John Montgomery.

Julia Montgomery dressed up for a costume party in Turkey.

From Mount St. Helena To Mosques and Minarets

WHEN JOHN AND I MARRIED in April 1948, we were no different from many other young couples starting out after World War II. Before I arrived, John had settled into a house in the new development of Wenachee Prairie (11 miles from Centralia and six miles from Chehalis, Washington). It was a five-room contemporary, paneled throughout with knotty pine and with a wood-burning fireplace, for the modest rent of $50 per month. The setting was exactly as John had described it in letters—"Ah, Wilderness!" There were evergreens, snow-capped mountains, and a trout stream rippling past our backyard, 75 yards from the house. We were in the heart of apple country, halfway between Seattle and Portland, Oregon. In spring when I arrived, the Wenachee Valley was aglow with the Apple Blossom Festival. It wasn't Munich, but I consoled myself with the sweeping view of Mount St. Helena through our picture window. John began putting in a lawn, and I soon discovered that cooking was my favorite domestic art.

When I arrived in the Far West, I didn't see that I would fit in—anywhere. I liked the friendly and open people, but when

I tried to find a job in personnel, with all the men home after the war, good positions for women were rare. I signed up for special courses in social work, and finally landed a job as probation officer at the Washington State School for Delinquent Girls. I traveled the circuit from Wenachee to Spokane—the first month, I logged over 2,000 miles! A fringe benefit of the job was the fruit I collected from the orchards I drove by— apples, blueberries, and pears—to preserve on weekends.

There were some 60 teenaged girls on my list of probationers, and I had to check on each one of them every three months. Many were Native Americans; all came from dysfunctional families. The girls matured young, nearly all were wild and unsupervised, had problems with sex. (Child abuse wasn't understood or talked about much in those days.)

When there were severe emotional problems, the standard solution at that time was the electric-shock treatment. I was the person who had to take the unfortunate girls to State Hospital. I didn't like it, but I felt that I had no choice. There were dramatic scenes; the families blamed me—with good reason. This method of treatment has since been replaced by drugs and psychotherapy. I would never have survived those difficult years without an understanding supervisor, Mary Hazen, a psychologist very advanced in her thinking. She gave me good on-the-job training, and told me to hang in there. This was especially hard to do after I broke my ankle in a freak accident at Sun Valley and had to drive all those miles in a cast!

I soon settled into the life of the community, becoming involved with local groups and activities. I was elected to membership in Sigma Chapter of the honorary society, Delta Kappa Gamma. The Altrusa and Business and Professional Women's Clubs discovered I had a gift for gab and asked me to give talks at meetings and dinners. When the Altrusa convention met in Portland, I was invited to give the ten-minute response to Mayor Dorothy McCullough Lee's welcoming address.

My speech-making was beginning to pay small dividends. I got $20 for one talk, and gave it away for family birthdays— one half to my father, the other half to my brother Ed. "Aren't we all getting old?" I wrote to Dad. (He was celebrating his 56th, I my 26th!) John predicted if I kept on making speeches, I'd be elected Congresswoman on my 30th.

While I was commuting around the area, John headed the Washington State National Guard in Takoma. He was also present at the organizational meeting of the local branch of UNESCO and elected chairman of the Lewis County chapter. He began working at the community level for that international body.

Those were very busy days for John and me. My workday started at 6 A.M. In a letter to my parents, I complained that we had not had one week-night at home together for three weeks! Both of us were chronic students. I was taking shorthand, John studying German. He was at work till midnight Monday and Thursday; I was away Tuesdays and Wednesdays. We were still on a strict budget trying to buy a house. Nonetheless, I was convinced that marriage to John was the right decision for me. John was a hard worker, and NO complaints. "I couldn't have gotten a better husband if I had him made to order," I wrote to my parents. "He'll do anything and everything for me."

We put our anniversary money into the bank for vacations. In May, we took a holiday with four other couples to Long Beach, Washington. We went crabbing and clamming and swimming, just being lazy before John headed off to National Guard summer camp in June.

When our lives were beginning to settle into a peaceful routine, we were awakened one night by what sounded like a locomotive roaring through the house. Lamps swayed, the

From Mount St. Helena To Mosques and Minarets

walls shook, the power went out. Growing up in Ohio, I had never felt anything like that. It frightened me; but John, who was raised in California, recognized the tremors. I had experienced my first earthquake! With good luck, no major damage was done to the house. I sent photos home to reassure the family that it wasn't as disastrous as the newspapers would have them believe.

Also about this time, John's mother came to live with us. John was the only child of Helen Consuelo Montgomery whose father, a promising young Cuban doctor, came to the U.S. in 1914 to join the Mayo Clinic. (On her mother's side, she often reminded us, she was descended from the Revolutionary War hero, General Anthony Wayne. We never knew how much of Helen's background was fact or fiction.) After a typical American childhood in Minnesota, Helen was one of the pioneer women to enroll at the University of California at Berkeley. She was a free spirit on an unconventional campus. When her traditional father heard that she was attending University dances *unchaperoned*, he ordered her home. In rebellion, still in her teens, Helen told us, she eloped with 50-year-old George Montgomery, scion of a prominent San Francisco jeweler's family (after which Montgomery Street was named). Helen was only 25 when she acknowledged her mistake and divorced George.

John was the only child of this union, so he and his mother were always close. Helen came to Centralia, happy to be near her only son and to putter around our garden. She promised to help with the housework while I was on the job.

In December 1948, I was invited to return to Munich for the anniversary of Friendship House. James Kelly, then military government area commander, was on hand to congratulate "Miss Peggy." In his opening remarks at the celebration, Jim called Friendship House "one of the really fine, positive things done for German girls by American women." It was my reward for a year of very hard work. Jean Gauthier, another State Department employee, had taken over my job and was carrying on with a smoothly-functioning organization. What more could anyone ask?

By this time, after several years of domesticity in Washington State, John and I were thinking more and more of the good years in Munich. He decided to reactivate his commission in the regular Army and to apply for military attaché training. The benefits were many: the possibility of seeing more of the world, and the security of retirement at age 53 at ⅔ pay—the munificent sum of $275 per month (more than hometown Ohio boys could make for a month's hard work)!

In June 1949, I announced to my anxious parents that they were "on the verge of being grandparents...I am feeling the kicking of little feet." John was reading up on child psychology and prenatal care. We planned to have the child baptized in the Catholic faith, and I asked my brother Ed, then taking a graduate degree in engineering at UCLA, to be godfather. When I wrote the good news to Jane Heether, my former apartment-mate in Munich, I got a lovely letter back. Of course, she was pleased. I was sure that Janie would like to marry and settle down too, but so far the right man had not come along. I wrote that "marriage is sort of a challenge— wonderful, but requiring the very best of everything one has... I do hope [you] take the step soon. It's a marvelous adventure."

John Edward Montgomery, our first-born, was delivered on October 14, 1949, at the hospital in Centralia, Washington. He was a healthy baby, and I took great pride and joy in nursing him. The next summer, when Mary Hazen sent me to a conference for social workers in Atlantic City, I dropped Johnny off in Akron for a first visit with his grandparents.

The Montgomerys were hoping to be posted near Ft. Knox, Kentucky, closer to my family, but our next move was to the eucalyptus-scented Monterey Peninsula. John was assigned to the Army's Advanced Language Training School at Fort Ord, California, to study Turkish, which gave us a hint of what our next assignment might be.

I adjusted to my new role as Army wife, too busy raising a family to regret my aborted career. John was not quite two when our second son, Stephen George, was born on February 7, 1951, in the Ft. Ord Station Hospital. I became involved in groups of other young wives centered around the Officers' Club. Our base housing was near China Beach on the edge of the beautiful Pacific, but the waves were too high, the water too cold for us. Only the hardiest beach boys in wet suits dared to venture into the ocean, so I took my little ones for a daily swim in the Officers' Club pool.

After a year at Ft. Ord, the powers-that-be decided John had learned enough of the language; he must also study the politics and history of the region before being shipped off to Turkey as military attaché. September 1951 found the Montgomerys crossing the continent again to the East Coast, trading eucalyptus for stately elms, Mission-style for neo-Gothic buildings. John's new assignment was the Middle East Institute at Princeton University, headed by the world-renowned Dr. Philip Hitti.

We arrived at that typical college campus on a brilliant fall afternoon with trees ablaze in red and gold, the air smelling of wood fires. Undergraduates were riding their bicycles on the old Quadrangle near historic Nassau Hall and the Firestone Library. New York City was just a short hour away.

With a growing family, we couldn't afford to live in Princeton township. A carriage house in Lawrenceville near the Ivy League prep school became available, and it sounded just right for us. There would be plenty of space for the boys to explore. We didn't know until later that our new home was on the estate of Junius P. Morgan, son of the famous financier. Recently divorced, Morgan arranged for his ex-wife to live in one-half of the cottage; the Montgomerys were offered the other half for a modest rent we could afford.

We were at Princeton for only one school term, but we enjoyed every minute. I settled in as resident Mom of the two boys, while John attended classes at the Institute. I filled my days making the rounds of the greengrocer's and the butcher's, pushing the boys' stroller at a leisurely pace down Nassau Street. I dawdled at bookshops and window-shopped along the way, picking up supplies at old-fashioned stores with fruit and vegetables stacked high in pyramids. I stopped to discuss the weather while the butcher operated on my slim cut of meat. This quiet university town was a mecca for intellectuals who had fled Nazi Germany during the 1930s and 1940s; it was not unusual to pass Albert Einstein on the street, looking like someone's grandfather, snacking on an ice-cream cone with neighborhood children following in his wake.

There were concerts and lectures, and when Helen followed us East to "sit" with the boys, we took in cultural events in New York we had not been able to enjoy yet. Though the budget wouldn't stretch for many such trips, when we could get away we hopped aboard the "Toonerville Trolley" to Princeton Junction connecting with the train into Manhattan, then rushed to catch the last one home from Penn Station before midnight.

In May, John was finishing his work at the Institute. He wrote his dissertation on the growing problems the U.S. would have with a pro-Israeli foreign policy and the dependence on Arab oil. (John was often one step ahead of his time, but since his subject was not considered relevant in the 1950s, he got a poor grade.)

As soon as John could get away, we left Princeton to spend the summer in Ohio with my family. It was important for the boys to know their grandparents. Many old friends dropped by to inspect the Army man Peggy Curry married. The *Beacon-*

Journal sent a reporter to write about us and our assignment to exotic Turkey. In early August, John went to Washington, D.C. for final briefings, while I stayed behind with the boys. Then on August 23, the four Montgomerys took the train to New York to board the ship for Istanbul.

This was the first stage of a slow, 21-day voyage across the Atlantic through the Mediterranean Sea to the Bosphorus. It was a smooth crossing, and no one became seasick. All of us enjoyed the long lazy days on the ocean, especially the boys, who had never seen such a big boat before. They frightened us one night when they left their bunks to explore the decks and appeared in the dining room in their Rudolph-the-Red-Nosed-Reindeer pajamas. I was terrified when I stopped to think where they might have wandered before they arrived at the table!

❧ II

A wife doesn't ask what her husband's duties as Military Attaché will be, but I knew that John was trained as a G-2 [Intelligence] Officer. Because of its strategic location, Turkey has always been a potential trouble spot. Only 15 minutes from Soviet territory, the fortress city of Erzurum had fallen twice to Russian invaders in the past 75 years. At the time we arrived, it was the headquarters of Turkey's Third Army, which the U.S. helped to train and equip. We soon found out that the Turkish people traditionally hate and fear the "Moskofs." There is an old Turkish saying that the only way a Moskof can get to Istanbul is to buy a ticket on the Orient Express!

Thanks to U.S. military aid, the Turks at that time had Europe's second largest standing army (Russia had No. 1). Turkish landing fields put the U.S. Air Force an hour away by jet from the Baku oil fields of Russia. Some 450,000 soldiers of the Turkish army, equipped with tanks and jet aircraft, were standing by to guard the free world's southern flank.

The city of Ankara had risen suddenly on the Anatolian plateau in 1923, when Mustafa Kemal Ataturk moved the government from Istanbul and transformed several formerly obscure villages into a modern capital of some 300,000 people. Ataturk Boulevard stretched from the Roman citadel on the hilltop to the Turkish White House (The Kosk) on the plain. The Boulevard was lined by contemporary public buildings and embassies and bordered by transplanted trees.

John's office was in the stark U.S. Embassy building on Ankara's main street. When George McGhee, the tall, distinguished Texan who was then U.S. Ambassador, looked out over the green plains, he was quoted as saying: "You know what this country reminds me of? It's got the stuff, the git up and go, and it's rolling. Why, Turkey today is just like Texas in 1919!" (Slightly larger than Texas, it was then No. 4 in wheat exports.)

Once known as "the sick man of Europe," Turkey had become—in one generation—the Middle East's most modern state, thanks to Ataturk. In the 1950s, it remained stable, strong and progressive under the leadership of Celal Bayar, an able banker who had followed Ataturk as President. There were still some isolated villages of mud huts, but Turkey seemed to be heading toward free enterprise and democratic government.

The Montgomerys settled into a spacious villa on the side of a hill with a beautiful view. The owner lived in an apartment on the second floor, the Montgomerys on first, and the devoted couple we hired to help us out, Ali-bey Hassan and his wife Neji-bey, were installed on the ground floor. Ali-bey did the yard work and other odd jobs around the place, and Neji-bey hovered over the primitive stove to produce the delicious lamb shish kebabs, couscous and rice, lentil stews and eggplant dishes that are staples of the Middle Eastern diet.

I located a nursery school for the boys, where Turkish and American kids played together in harmony, save for the squabbles all kids are subject to, anytime, anywhere. (Before we left

Ankara our oldest, John, spoke perfect Turkish.) One of our first holiday celebrations was "Children's Day," an annual event with Boy and Girl Scouts on parade, parties, free movies and President Bayar's visit to selected schools.

With a live-in sitter at home for the children, I had time to take on another job. The Fulbright program was just setting up in Ankara, and I was hired as executive secretary of the U.S. Educational Commission. I liked working in personnel again, interviewing Turks who wanted to go to the U.S., and reviewing applications of American students and professors seeking grants to study in Turkey. My desk was in the PAO (Public Affairs) office, within walking distance of the house. The hours were 9 to 1 o'clock according to local custom, followed by a long leisurely lunch, then back to the office from 3 to 5.

During our years in Ankara, I was an active member of the Turkish-American Women's Cultural Society. As secretary of the Society and co-chairman of the literature group, I made many lasting friendships. It amused my friends when I walked down the aisle in a borrowed Turkish officer's uniform, complete with mustache, for one of their costume parties.

To my amazement, in this country where women had worn veils so recently, great progress was being made. Turkey became a model for other Middle Eastern countries. Women not only held important jobs in government, but were shop assistants, clerks, telephone operators. In the 1950s, any girl who wanted a job could get one, and at the same rate of pay as a man.

This amazing change began with the Westernization movement of Ataturk in the 1920s and continued under the Democratic Party leadership of President Bayar. Before he departed for the U.S. on a goodwill tour in 1954, Bayar visited the Embassy. Someone suggested it would be good public relations to photograph the President with an American staff member, and Mrs. John Montgomery was the one chosen.

I remember the black suit, pink blouse, and little black hat that I wore that day, but I'm ashamed I can't remember anything the President said. (Some years later, in a May 1960 coup d'etat by army officers, Bayar and his prime minister, Adnan Menderes, were ousted from office and condemned to death. Bayar's life was spared because of his ill health and old age, but Menderes was executed.)

Julia Montgomery with Cecil Bayar, President of Turkey in 1954.

Our tour of duty in Turkey was a peaceful one—no coups or revolutions. We celebrated our first Christmas in Ankara as we did at home. (We were disappointed it wasn't white. The Anatolian plateau is baked by sun in the summer, springlike in fall and winter.) To my surprise, Turkey followed many U.S. customs. Some Turkish families put up Christmas trees, and many of our Moslem friends exchanged greeting cards.

The Ankara Golf Club was the social center of Ankara. The Montgomerys were invited to celebrate New Year's Eve with its members at the beautiful Swedish Legation residence. Mrs. Croneberg, the Swedish Minister's wife, headed the receiving line, along with the Turkish Minister of Foreign Affairs,

Professor Koprulu, the Minister of Spain, the Italian Ambassador, and other high-ranking members of the diplomatic corps and their wives. John was decked out in full dress uniform and I, for that special occasion, wore formal evening dress. (My party best was a pale contrast to the vivid red sari with golden border worn by Chandra Shekar, the Indian Ambassador's wife.)

Another memorable evening, for different reasons, was at the home of the U.S. Consul General, Colonel John Gay. My indomitable mother-in-law, Helen Montgomery, had arrived

Julia and John Montgomery with the Turkish Foreign Minister Kropulu and his wife (far right) in Ankara, Turkey, New Year's Eve party, 1954.

after six months for a visit. She had not been in Ankara long when we hustled her off to a dinner party with us at the Gays. Helen, a near teetotaler, celebrated with several glasses of wine. We had not warned her that high altitude causes alcohol to go to one's head. Helen was the life of the party that night, but John had been afraid her performance might wreck his career!

Our next guest was John's greatly admired professor, Dr. Philip Hitti from Princeton. He was a walking encyclopedia on a field trip to the old Turkish settlements on the Anatolian plain. The Turks swept in from the open steppes in the 11th century and settled on the ruins of half a dozen civilizations. Nomadic herders were still sleeping on the ground in tents, or living in windswept villages in huts made of dung and mud, just as their ancestors had done for centuries. We saw Hittite figures carved on the cliff face in the Tarsus foothills, and the Roman gate in Tarsus dating back to the days of St. Paul.

We often explored the historic sites of Istanbul, an eight-hour drive from Ankara. I went there to meet exchange students and professors arriving from the U.S. My first glimpse was disappointing—reddish-brick walls in narrow, unpaved streets lined with squalid houses and shops—like any other Third World country. But when we crossed the Golden Horn with the Sea of Marmara glimmering on our right and came into the heart of the old city (dating back to Mohammed the Conquerer in 1452), I was suitably impressed. The grandeur of the Blue Mosque, Santa Sophia, and Top Kapi were reminders of the days when Istanbul was capital of a mighty empire. We often returned with an inexpensive treasure from the great covered bazaar. For dinner, we liked to stop at our favorite Greek restaurant in Therapia, where live five-to-ten-pound lobsters were harvested from a water tank in the center of the room and displayed to the customers before cooking.

The leading hotel, the Park, had a fine band for dancing. It was a notorious hangout for the OSS and other intelligence services during World War II. During the war, Istanbul was an asylum for refugees from Bulgaria, Rumania, and other Iron Curtain countries, so the Soviet Union as well as the U.S. considered it an important source of information. (At the Park, in August 1945, a top Soviet intelligence officer, Konstantin

Volkov, defected to the British, with Kim Philby handling the negotiations in London.)

III

In June of our third summer in Turkey, we drove our old Dodge through Europe on a long-awaited vacation. Dot Case, my former New York roommate, was visiting us in Ankara and went along for the ride on the first part of the trip. Dottie was a great traveler, wonderful with the boys and always pleasant and interesting with John and me.

The first two nights after Istanbul we stopped in Thessaloniki, a typical Greek city on the Aegean Sea, surrounded by hills. We feasted on *dolmaides* and *baklava* washed down with *retsina* in a restaurant overlooking the waterfront. The next day we detoured to Piraeus to enjoy the beaches, and then on to Athens to show the boys the Parthenon and the other majestic ruins on the Acropolis. From Greece it was a straight shoot up the coast to the rest of Europe.

We visited Sarajevo, the then-peaceful capital of Bosnia. The focus of headline news again in the 1990s, Sarajevo was the scene of the assassination of the Austrian Archduke Franz Ferdinand in 1914 that sparked off World War I. (The place across the river by the bridge from which the Serbian assassin fired the fateful shot is marked by a footprint in the pavement.) Many of its finest buildings date back to the 15th century, when Sarajevo was an important military and administrative center under the Turks. The hills rise steeply on both sides of the rushing Miljacka river which runs through the center of town. On the lower slopes, the domes and minarets of the mosques and red-tiled roofs of the old Turkish houses stand out against a green background of gardens and trees. Hemmed in on three sides by mountains, a new city with office blocks was just beginning to rise above the Moslem quarter.

From Sarajevo, the valley of the Neretva runs directly down to the Adriatic. We drove from Split along the beautiful Dalmatian Coast on a well-maintained post-World War II highway to Dubrovnik, the walled city. Dubrovnik could be entered only by one of several fortified gates. No cars were allowed, so we parked outside and explored the city on foot. Old Dubrovnik is an interesting assortment of tall, narrow buildings with red or brown-tiled roofs, palaces, domed churches, shops, towers and small squares, with an impressive baroque cathedral built in the late 17th century on the site of an earlier Romanesque building destroyed by a great earthquake. The old Placa remains almost unchanged after some three or four hundred years. The clock tower at the end of the square was lighted at night, and we had great fun promenading up and down with the locals.

We drove on to Zagreb, passing through tidy villages and farms with well-cultivated fields, well-kept barns and orchards and vineyards. We could see the great castles of the Hapsburgs and other noble families, for the most part ruined or empty, on the hilltops. A friend from Munich days, Howard Goldsmith, was Consul General at that time in Zagreb. He booked a room for us in a hotel reserved for U.S. Embassy employees, and kept us up half the night reminiscing.

Zagreb's broad tree-lined avenues and handsome 19th century buildings reminded us that we were getting closer to Western Europe. There were theaters, an opera house, galleries and sidewalk cafes where one could sit and sip cups of thick coffee topped with double cream. The twin Gothic spires of St. Stephen's Cathedral and the brightly-colored roof of the Church of St. Mark's towered above this devoutly Catholic city. I am thankful that I had an opportunity to see these places before the terrible destruction of the civil war.

We crossed the Iron Curtain enroute to Vienna, and John barked orders to the boys not to make the usual racket in the back seat. Someone had to go to the bathroom every few miles, first Johnny, then Stephen, then Johnny again, then Stephen. When John pulled over to the side of the road, he told them to make it quick!

Vienna was recovering from the Allied bombing during the war. The beautiful Opera House received a direct hit in March 1945. It was still a shell, with most of the interior burned out. Even among the ruins, there was no escaping the majesty of that great city. An outdoor restaurant with sawdust floor had sprung up in the shadow of St. Stephen's Cathedral. But the treasures of the Imperial Palace of Schönbrunn, hidden for safety in a salt mine during the War, were restored to their original site. It was a comfortable "home," and seemed as if Queen Maria Theresa and her family had just gone away for a weekend and would soon return.

I'm sure the boys enjoyed most riding on the gigantic ferris wheel U.S. movie-goers of the era may remember from the film, *The Third Man*. I added a few pounds at the Hotel Sacher, home of the world famous tortes. John and I also spent an evening at the Grinzing *weinstube*, eating savory sausages and sampling newly fermented wine while enjoying the sing-along. All of us said goodbye to Vienna reluctantly.

The next night we arrived in the tiny duchy of Luxembourg, another medieval walled city, then drove on to Munich. Along the way we stopped at Regensburg, the town that John had "liberated" with General Patton at the end of the war, then the site of a school for U.S. Army officers studying the Russian language.

When we got to Paris, we checked into the Hotel St. Romain near the Tuileries Gardens. Our top-floor room had a spectacular view, but the boys frightened us when they insisted on hanging out the windows. (Stephen always threatened to push John off high places!) Never too young, I thought, to introduce children to the great works of art at the Louvre.

But our kids were much more interested in the Gardens with the carousel than in the great art masterpieces.

After leaving Dot in the flower-filled city of Cannes on the French Riviera, we traveled leisurely along the Italian coast, stopping in Pisa to see the Leaning Tower. (The boys thought it was sensational. We took photos of them trying to hold it up, and once again, Stephen threatened to push John over the top!).

Dot had made reservations for us at the Gran Hotel in Rome, so we moved right in. Imagine my surprise to see Bob Byer, a good friend I worked with in Ankara. He invited us to explore his favorite sights in the Eternal City that evening. The next day, we met a friend from Munich days, Carl Thomas, in the lobby of the American Embassy building. He gave us the "grand tour," and the boys tossed coins in the Trevi Fountain so we would be sure to return.

We had to hurry back to Naples before our leave was up. I held my breath as John skirted the hairpin curves on the spectacular Amalfi Drive. Then we headed into the port city to catch the car ferry back to Istanbul.

John was scheduled to fly to Beirut on July 1, while the boys and I returned to Ankara to close the house. We would be in Lebanon about six weeks, while John attended a Department of State seminar at the American University. Our good friends, the Ashfords, offered to drive to Beirut with the boys and me, so we didn't have to make the trip alone.

In the halcyon days of the 1950s, before hostages were taken and that city became a battleground, Beirut was a garden spot known as the Paris of the Middle East. It was famous for its cedar-lined Corniche. In contrast to our house in land-locked Ankara, the vast Mediterranean stretched out in front of our apartment building. From the 8th floor balcony over-looking the harbor, we could watch the water skiers and sun-bathers on the beach below.

The boys were four- and six-years-old, big enough to take them with a picnic lunch to one of the beautiful coves with rock formations a few miles south of town. Some members of the Embassy staff rented beach houses, and on weekends our family would go there to swim with friends or eat at one of the seafood restaurants opposite Pigeon Rocks.

The landmark St. George Hotel was a beautiful sight, built on a cliff overhanging the water. We sipped drinks on the terrace and watched fishing boats head out to sea at sunset. The St. George was also known for people-watching. Possibly John was keeping an eye on the nearby Phalange Club on the water's edge, where important political figures congregated.

The religious factor dominates Lebanese society and politics in that divided country. Since 1943, when Lebanon became independent from Syria, a power-sharing ratio was established among the many warring factions: the President was a Maronite, a member of the large Christian community; the Prime Minister, a Sunni Moslem; the Speaker of Parliament, a Shiite. Cabinet positions were filled by members of other major sects—the Greek Orthodox, the Greek Catholic, the Druze, and non-Semitic ethnic groups, such as the Kurds. When Lebanon joined the Arab League in 1945, the Maronites refused to accept it, and the seeds of the current troubles were sown. One can imagine the many problems studied by an apolitical U.S. military attaché in that explosive country!

At the end of the seminar, the boys and I went back to Turkey for three weeks, while John joined a conducted tour of Near Eastern capitals. Then on September 8, we took the boat together to the U.S. and headed straight for Ohio. Tired and a bit worse for the wear, we looked forward to settling in for a few weeks at home.

We were waiting for John's orders to come through. After living overseas for four years, surrounded by so much history and exotic customs, we got the news that we would be assigned to the USA again: Washington, D.C., would be our next home.

❧ IV

In my early thirties, if someone had told me I would make a considerable fortune as a stockbroker, I would have thought it impossible. I was an Army wife and mother. When John got his orders, the migrant Montgomery family folded its tents like the Arabs and returned to the U.S. to live. We settled down in a two-story white-brick house furnished from scratch on Greenbriar Street off Lee Highway in Arlington, Virginia, then far-out suburbia. In April 1955 our third son, Michael Curry Montgomery, was born at the U.S. Army Hospital at Ft. Belvoir.

In the mid-1950s, our family got by on $40 a week. There was never enough money, and I longed for a chance to do something not connected with diapers, formula, and refereeing boyish squabbles. I thought I might as well learn how to stretch an Army officer's paycheck to keep up with our grow-ing family. I signed up for a graduate correspondence course in Investment and Security Analysis conducted by the New York University Institute of Finance and received a certificate in June 1956.

Then I discovered that George M. Ferris, Jr., vice president of a local brokerage firm founded by his father, was teaching a course in securities and investment at George Washington University. I hurried across the bridge to enroll. After several weeks in class, Ferris observed that I had a real feel for the business. He gave me an aptitude test, the kind that predicts whether or not a person will be successful in that field, and to my surprise, I made an exceptionally high score. I asked George for a desk in the sales department at Ferris & Company, and he went out on a limb and offered me a job as apprentice stockbroker.

Like other dutiful wives of the time, I asked my husband's advice, whether or not I should take it. "They're not going to pay me anything," I told John. "They'll just give me a desk and a telephone. It's all on commission."

"That's O.K., doll," John agreed. "You'll learn a lot more on the battlefield than in the War College." (I was lucky to have a supportive husband.) "I'll take care of the bills for the first six months, then we'll take another look," he said. "It's probably the best investment we'll ever make."

In the long run, John was right, but it was a year before I showed any profit as the "token" woman in the office. By the time I figured what it cost for a maid to help out at home, travel expenses and clothes, it was actually costing me to work.

The men in the brokerage at that time weren't used to having a woman colleague in the front office. They took the attitude that I wasn't serious, just a flash in the pan. But I stuck it out, learned all I could about the business. Six months later, I passed the exam and became a registered broker on the New York Stock Exchange. My husband continued to believe in me until I came home with my first $1,000 commission. To celebrate, I invited my office colleagues out for drinks. Two young men who were on my team from the beginning were Bob O'Neil and Duane Waldenburg. They were always there when I needed them, and wonderful with the boys on weekends.

With the little money we could save—in the beginning, only $25 per month—I began investing in stock. The first one I chose was Goodyear. The dust and dirt of the plant had filled my nose and eyes in early years but the company treated my family well, so I had faith in it.

When my first investments trebled in value, I sold out to buy a new car. That was my first big mistake, the one by which I learned my most important lesson in the business: hold your winners! If I had held on a little longer, my investment would have multiplied 20 times over.

Those were busy years, so busy with work and family there wasn't much time for anything else. My fourth boy, Mark Julian, was born in January 1957, and I went back to work three weeks later. We were up at 6:30 A.M. Monday through Friday. After feeding the family and bathing the baby, I digested the financial page of the paper with my breakfast coffee. Then we got the two older boys off to school before John left for the Pentagon and I commuted into downtown Washington. By the time I left the house at nine, I felt as if I'd lived a whole day.

Julia Montgomery with her fourth son, Mark Julian, born in January 1957.

We asked John's mother to stay with us again, as "assistant mother" to the babies. She had done such a good job in bringing up John, I was sure she would do the same with our sons. I went home after 4:30, when the market closed, read to the boys, played games, or helped with homework until dinner. Thursday night, we did the marketing. The biggest item on the list was milk—24 quarts of it! Saturday night was the only time John and I had alone, to party with Army friends or go to spaghetti dinners at someone's home. Sunday was reserved for the children, a time all of us enjoyed exploring the many historic sites of the nation's capital.

From Mount St. Helena To Mosques and Minarets

I have always felt more at home in the stock market than in the supermarket. I soon became so successful in advising clients that I was asked to share this knowledge with others. The Washington branch of the American Association of University Women wanted me to take over their course in money management. I began to organize seminars at the YWCA evenings and Saturdays for people who knew almost nothing about investments. On typical weeknights, after dinner with the family and tucking the boys into bed, I headed for one women's group or another. I soon found myself teaching four nights and two afternoons a week. In those days, the markets were still open on Saturdays, and the clients coming in on Saturday A.M. made business better. (I learned another valuable lesson: educating clients is good for business, and if you do well for your clients, you do well for yourself.)

Just as I was making a name for myself in my new career, the fates stepped in again. In the summer of 1957, John came home with the news that he was being transferred to the Army Staff School at Ft. Riley, Kansas. In October, we made a farewell trip to Hot Springs, Virginia (near the Homestead), on the birthday weekend (John's on October 11, our son John's on the 14th). Young John still remembers floating around lazily in the warm, swirling water, and that his often serious, tense father was relaxed and happy for a very brief time.

When the Montgomerys put their house up for sale, there were no takers. John had to go, and I stayed behind to show the place and to close out my job and my classes. Those were very rough months for me, mentally and physically. I tried to do too much, and my health, which was usually good, suffered. I spent five weeks in bed with pneumonia, but finally got back on my feet, weak and exhausted. By December, I managed to sell the house and say goodbye to my clients.

It was hard to leave the job at the brokerage firm I had finally found a niche in, but like any dutiful Army wife,

I "paid, packed and followed." On the Friday before Christmas, I was on the road again with the boys—John, 8; Stephen, 6; Michael, 2½; and the baby Mark, just 11-months-old, in the car seat beside me.

The boys were fretful and sniffling with colds when we pulled up in front of my mother's place in Akron. I was glad to collapse and to let their grandmother feed and take charge of them. I had noticed an ominous knock under the hood of the old car we were then driving early that morning. I couldn't risk another day on the highway with the boys until we checked it out. The next morning, Sunday, I called the owner of the nearby service station and asked him to send a tow truck.

"Ya gotta be kiddin', lady. The mechanics have gone home. I'm closin' up for Christmas."

Not to worry. John would understand. He always did. When I got him on the phone to repeat the bad news, he said stoically, "That's all right, doll. I'll eat my turkey at the Officers' Club." (Remembering World War II, I knew this would not be the first lonely Christmas of John's life.) "Don't you worry, doll. Stay right there with your mother until you're sure the old bus is safe. I don't want anything to happen to you and the boys," he said. Then, "I love you," and he rang off. Those were the last words John said to me.

It was December 23, 1957. When the phone rang again, even before I heard the words from that grave voice, I sensed something was terribly, terribly wrong.

"Mrs. Montgomery," the voice said. "This is the chaplain at Ft. Riley. I am sorry, Mrs. Montgomery, to call you at this time, but there has been an accident. I have very sad news for you."

I blocked out most of that conversation and everything else that happened that night. My first thought was, what shall I tell the boys? Tomorrow is Christmas Eve. The two younger ones would be too young to understand, but John and Stephen?

On Christmas Eve morning, I told the older boys, as gently as I could, that there had been an accident on field maneuvers, and their father would never come back. They were too young to fully comprehend, but they understood enough to remember this moment for the rest of their lives. When it came time to open the presents, each wanted a remembrance of their father. John and Stephen started scuffling over his gift, the pen and pencil set I had so carefully wrapped with the card enclosed: "To John, with love."

The actual circumstances of the "accident" are still unclear. The Statement of Death listed the cause as "Gunshot Wound," but considering the depth of John's depression, I feared that the wound might have been self-inflicted. The year before, he had made a new will, with myself and the children as principal beneficiaries. John Montgomery was a true hero who received high praise for courage under fire in wartime. He was recognized by his commanding officers for exceptional qualities of leadership, ability and intelligence. The uninspiring routine of civilian life, his high aspirations and his unreasonable fear of failure brought on the crippling depression that may have caused him to take his own life.

My mother went with us to Kansas to arrange for John's body to be sent back to Washington, and Helen joined us there as soon as she heard the sad news. Lt. Colonel Charles Mead, commanding officer of the 69th Armored Division, wrote to me afterwards: "…under the circumstances, it was a distinct honor to meet you and your family as well as John's mother. You are constantly in our thoughts, and we of John's Squadron send you our blessings."

Our dear friend Mac MacCormac, now living in San Francisco, was standing by when most needed. He had introduced me to John, and remained our good friend during our courtship and the early years of our marriage. He flew to Ohio to meet us at my mother's home and drove with us back to Washington.

Fellow officers and friends sent their messages of condolence from posts around the world. Our friend "Rollie" Kolb, a colonel on the staff of the Joint U.S. Military Mission for Aid to Turkey, spoke for many when he wrote: "the news… came as a great shock to Billie [his wife] and me. It is very difficult for us to realize that such a thing could happen to such a wonderful person."

John was buried in Section 30 of Arlington National Cemetery with full military honors. When the silent servicemen folded the flag that covered John's coffin neatly into a triangle and handed it to me, I knew my role as Army wife was over.

Julia with the four Montgomery boys (Stephen, Mark, John and Michael).

CHAPTER FOUR

From Widowhood To Wall Street

EVERYONE REMARKED how quickly I pulled myself together after John's death. They didn't know I was in a state of walking shock. My Catholic faith sustained me, and anger at the unfairness of it gave me an added boost of energy. I had the boys to think about. Though my world was collapsing, I couldn't let them down. But what should I do with my left-over life? Could I earn enough so that the boys and I could live comfortably?

I decided to stay in the Washington area where I had friends and, I hoped, a job. I thought of re-entering the Foreign Service, but the government turned me down. The mother of four small boys is not a likely candidate to send to an overseas post. New York was another possibility; an entry-level job there would lead to more success in my chosen field. But it meant commuting, a 60-hour week, and not enough time or emotional energy left over for the boys. I was pleased when George Ferris offered to take me back.

At that time, I wasn't in any emotional state to meet the public. I had to get my family settled first. The Army stood by us. Major Lilly and Colonel Rigel, two of John's fellow officers, arranged for the shipment of our household goods and John's personal effects back from Kansas. But it was up to me to organize my new life. Fortunately my mother-in-law agreed to stay with us. While I worked to supplement my Army widow's pension, she promised to take care of the boys.

A new idea came to me that I heartily recommend to other working mothers. I offered to give Helen 20 percent of everything I made after taxes, to provide a pension plan, health benefits, profit-sharing and vacation time for her, like any other valuable and important wage earner. You can't pay someone enough to sit up all night with a sick child.

For her part, Helen felt useful, a member of the team, a full "partner." How can I describe Helen? She was not the conventional grey-haired grandmother, who baked cookies and read bedtime stories to the children. She was a stylish, sophisticated woman, very contemporary in looks and outlook. She caused heads to turn whenever she walked down Connecticut Avenue, dressed to the nines for a casual lunch with one of her friends. The bedtime stories she read to the boys were often taken from Greek mythology—or the Old Testament. She was devout in her faith, but bounced around from one religion to another, from Christianity to Buddhism. The great love of her life was her only son, and after he was gone, his four little boys.

With these early decisions made, I rented a house on Greenwich Parkway in the District and tried to concentrate on earning a living. When John died, he left me with $880.14 in the bank, a 1954 Oldsmobile 4-door sedan valued at $1,086, and paid-up insurance policies worth $41,329. In addition, the stocks I had invested in had grown to a nest egg of $14,000 by December 1957, among them IT&T, Shell, and Amerada Petroleum. My mother turned over to me the Goodyear Tire & Rubber stock she had held onto for so long.

The readjustment period was expensive, as well as painful. We went through most of my savings in just three months. I didn't earn much at first, but my former clients at Ferris & Company finally came back, and soon I was able to provide more than just food and necessities for the family.

With the proceeds from John's insurance policies plus my early conservative investments in the market, Helen and I were able to pay $65,000 in cash for a spacious colonial house on Millwood Lane in northwest Washington in 1959. I lived there until 1993. I had moved around for so many years, the only thing I really wanted to own was a home.

✿ II

On March 1, 1959, I was made General Partner of Ferris & Company, the only woman partner of a New York Stock Exchange member firm in the Washington area. At that time, another special person came into my life, Jane Prentice. Jane started at the company as a floating secretary, and from the day I became partner, she was my personal secretarial assistant. She has been with me in one capacity or another since that time, with a few years off to marry and raise a family of her own. (She still works part-time for my son, Mark.)

With Jane's help, I started my classes again, and the list of clients grew. After dinner, we would meet downtown to set the room up and present the seminars. After the audience left, I would ask Jane, "How did it go?" or "How am I doing?" She would relay to me some of the participants' comments: "So much information in such a short time!" or, "She talks faster than I can listen!"

The long hours and stress of those years, the delayed shock over John's death, finally caught up with me. I worked too hard and tried to do too much. My way of coping was to deny the pain and just work harder, a coping strategy often employed by men.

Early one morning in 1959, I tried to get out of bed and fell back on the pillow, exhausted. Stephen, who was always eager to help, decided to bring me breakfast in bed. When I reached out to take the coffee pot, I knocked it out of his hands, all over my stomach. I never liked to go to doctors, always considered myself lucky to have a high energy level and reasonably good health. But with third-degree burns covering a large area of my body, I had to call for help.

March 1, 1959: Julia became the only woman General Partner of a New York Stock Exchange member firm in Washington.

When the doctor saw the extent of the damage, he wanted to send me to the hospital. I protested that I couldn't leave the house with four young boys. Stephen felt terrible, that it was all his fault. But he had probably saved me from an even greater catastrophe. Without the accident, the doctor would not have been called or noticed how gray my color was. When he tested my blood pressure and vital signs, he discovered I was in a terrible state of stress. He ordered bed rest for a week, without which, he warned, I was a sure candidate for a heart attack or stroke. Jane Prentice came to my rescue again. She maintained the office during the week. When Saturday came, Stephen was due at Georgetown Prep for an interview and to take the entrance exam. Jane piled all of the boys into my car and drove out to the school to drop him off. Then she came back to the house to help me with some office work before going back to the school again. I couldn't have made it through that difficult time without her help. Because of the accident, I learned one valuable lesson, to pamper myself and to take more time off.

The boys and I had some great times together in the early days of my widowhood. Stephen reminded me of the summer he and John went with me on a combined business and pleasure trip to California. We first stopped in L.A. to visit my brother, who graduated from UCLA in engineering and was then working at McDonnell Douglas Aircraft. Ed and his wife Betty invited us to their home in Santa Monica, so that my boys would get to know their cousins—Tim, Peter, Matthew, Chris, Eddie—and Katie, the only girl in the Curry/ Montgomery family.

Then to the kids' delight, we rented a turquoise Impala convertible and drove to San Francisco along the coastal highway, the scenic route, with the top down. Stephen and John were put on a "per diem" allowance of $5.00 for food; if one of them ate more than that, he had to take it out of his earnings! The boys especially liked to stop for "Banana Bonanzas," the huge, gloppy, Blum's version of a banana split. It was *my* treat if they finished every bite, *theirs* if they didn't.

My primary goal was to visit Hewlett-Packard in Palo Alto, the Wayne-Gossard Company, and the Grass Valley Group north of San Francisco in Sonoma. I recognized early the investment potential of emerging growth stocks in the area now known as "Silicon Valley." While I visited the companies on the Peninsula, the boys took the train back to D.C. via Chicago, with a stop-off at Las Vegas. (They've never told me about their adventures there.)

When they came home, I decided it would be good discipline for the fatherless boys to enter the all-male world of a military school. We tried the experiment first with John, the oldest, who was shipped off to Leonard Hall, the Navy preparatory school near Leonardtown, Maryland. In spite of the fact that families were allowed to visit every weekend, John cried when we left and was so miserable that when he finished out the year, we decided to let him come home. The strict discipline was a very valuable experience. John, who was a poor student before, began to excel when he entered the Priory School in Washington the next term. But we never threatened to send him—or any of the other boys—to a boarding school again.

In the spring, George Ferris recommended me for the Finance. I was the first woman to crack that all-male barrier. It was not easy for me. When I first went to Philadelphia, seats emptied out on either side whenever I appeared. But from that experience, I learned many valuable lessons about the investment business and about the interpersonal relationship-building process now known as "networking."

That summer, Ferris gave me time off for a trip to Europe to visit American companies in which our customers had investments. I wanted to take a look at how these companies operated abroad—their competition, background, and growth prospects. The markets in the rest of the world were expanding rapidly and the international aspects of business merited serious consideration.

I also thought it would be a valuable part of the children's education to share some of my travel experiences. I decided to take one of the boys along on each of my business trips. At that time Michael was five, and Mark, the baby, was always beating up on him. I thought it would be a good idea to separate the two youngest, to let Mark hold the center of Helen's attention while we were gone.

So Michael came with me to Switzerland, Portugal, Spain, Holland and Germany. He was a perfect love all the way.

Risks & Rewards

In Madrid, we stayed at the famous old Ritz Hotel and visited the Prado. I called on the International Telephone & Telegraph Company. With the world getting smaller faster, global telecommunications were just starting to accelerate, and IT&T was at the forefront of this new technology. I returned convinced that our company should take advantage of these new international investment opportunities.

We went on to Portugal, where one of our special memories was a visit to the Shrine of Fatima. We both loved the tram-car ride up to the Old City of Lisbon, where we listened to *fado* singers croon their mournful songs.

There were times I had to get baby-sitters, but in many cities we renewed old friendships with Foreign Service or Army families and they took over. In The Hague, we visited Mike Cavanaugh, then Consul General, for a look at the tulip industry. I discovered that tulips originated in Turkey and were brought back to the Netherlands in the 16th century by the Dutch Ambassador, who had seen tulips growing in Adrianople. In the early 17th century, the prices of tulips rose to unprecedented heights, creating a "tulip mania," which brought great wealth to Holland before the market collapsed.

Though the bulb fields are in full bloom in April and May, flowers are a year-round business in the Netherlands. The Bollenstreek Route is a special itinerary designed by the Dutch Auto Club through the heart of the flower-growing region. The route, marked with little blue and white signs, begins in Oegstgeest near Leiden, and circles through Rijnsburg (site of one of Holland's three major flower auction houses) and the beach communities of Katwijk and Noordwijk, Hillegom, Lisse (site of Keukenhof Gardens), and Sassenheim. Keukenhof is a 28-hectare (70 acre) park and greenhouse com-plex, planted each year in a special spring exhibition to intro-duce the newest hybrids developed by Dutch botanists.

It was an easy drive from Amsterdam to the small village of Aalsmeer, site of the famous flower auction held year round, five days a week, from before dawn until mid-morning. It is the largest flower auction in the world, with three halls continuously operating in a building the size of several football fields. We walked on a catwalk above the rolling four-tier carts that were waiting to move past the auctioneers. In a Dutch auction, the price goes down, not up, on a large "clock" on the wall, and the buyers sit lecture-style with buzzers on their desks; the first buyer to register a bid gets the bunch.

When I told Mike Cavanaugh I wanted to see the electronics show in Russia, to visit some of the potentially difficult Iron Curtain countries, he and his wife offered to keep Michael. I next visited Warsaw, where my old friend Francis Underhill was Consul General. The Central Hotel was run-down and dirty, but Frank rescued me from that grim place and gave a party for me. He also provided a car for the drive to Krakov, the industrial center. My tour of the Polish companies was made more interesting because of Frank's assistance and fluent use of the language.

My first visit to Russia was marked by an event recorded in history as the "U-2 Incident." Lt. Gary Powers, a U.S. Air Force pilot based in Turkey, was shot down on a reconnaissance mission over the Soviet Union. President Eisenhower, in Paris for a difficult Cold War summit with Nikita Khruschev, first denied the U-2 was on a spy mission, but no one was fooled, least of all the Russians. I read about it in an English-language newspaper the day after I arrived in Moscow. I found the story hard to believe, even before I heard, a few days later, that then-Secretary of State Christian Herter admitted Powers was on a spying mission. Powers' plane was exhibited in Gorky Park, and it was a tense time in Moscow for U.S. visitors. I was staying at the Metropole, the Intourist Hotel, where I suspected there were electronic "bugs" in every room, and I am positive my suitcase was searched.

Though the U-2 incident was still very much in the news during my stay in Moscow, there was no open hostility towards me personally, as an American citizen. I was seldom out-of-sight of my Intourist guide, but everywhere we went, I was greeted with friendliness and curiosity. I was impressed with the amount of new housing being built, enormous projects as far as the eye could see. I guess they were trying to catch up with what they lacked before. The progress the Russians made in some other areas fascinated me, especially the long-distance telephone equipment employing microwaves. It was obvious that there would be many investment opportunities in defense electronics in that country.

In the evening, I was on my own. I looked up my friend Forrest Davis, then Cultural Attaché at the U.S. Embassy. He helped me to get tickets to the enchanting puppet theater and the Russian Ballet, the finest in the world. One night, I decided to dress for dinner and go to a hotel where, according to rumor, one might see high-ranking Soviet leaders. I discovered that foreigners were welcome, but unescorted ladies were not. I was standing in the hotel entrance, wondering what to do, when an unknown Britisher came along and understood my plight. He took me by the arm, pretending to be an old friend, and whisked me into the dining room. We had a pleasant dinner together, and several other such evenings followed. This chance encounter greatly enhanced my enjoyment of Moscow. When I got back to Washington, my friends predicted that a romance might develop, but I pointed out that my British companion came up to my shoulder on the dance floor!

In the early days of my widowhood, I also traveled to South America for the first time. Gladys Baker, an old friend from Kent State, was then Labor Attaché at the U.S. Embassy in Caracas. I took that opportunity to visit Gladys and to explore the northeast coast of Venezuela, where iron ore was being processed by the U.S. Steel Company out of great canyons of solid rock. I also visited the vast oil fields of Lake Maracaibo, another source of wealth for that formerly underdeveloped country. There were major investment opportunities in Venezuela, not only in the production of oil, but in the export-import business.

My seminars on investing in U.S. markets were very popular in Latin American countries, where a woman stockbroker is an unusual spectacle. I had very little free time to use the swimming pool at the Tamanaco, the beautiful hotel built on the hillside overlooking the city, because of the hospitality of warm and simpático Venezuelan friends.

I did not return to South America until some 20 years later, when I went with Tom Walsh to an international conference in Rio de Janeiro. We stayed at the Copacabana Palace Hotel on Copacabana Beach, with a dramatic view of the Sugar Loaf from our window. It was hard not to relax and to forget the business in the warm sunshine of Rio, with beaches and beautiful people in the "city that care forgot"!

III

A turning point in my career came in February 1962, when Ferris & Company sent me to Cambridge, Massachusetts, to attend the Advanced Management Program of the Harvard Business School. It was hard to be away from the office and family for this length of time, but I tried to organize everything before I went. It was Stephen's turn to go with me to Boston. I enrolled him in the fifth grade at a school suggested by my Boston cousin, Jim Mooney. He failed to tell me that the Brothers of the Sharon Academy of the Sacred Heart were strict disciplinarians, accustomed to dealing with rough boys having problems at home. In spite of Stephen's good record, I'm sure he would have been delighted at any time to pack his bag and head back to Washington; but he was a good sport and stuck it out till the end of term.

I shall quote excerpts from a letter I wrote to my parents about the experience.

Dear Mom and Dad:

After almost three weeks, I must admit I am really snowed under… busy every minute, and worn out trying to be my sociable self and still get all I can out of the course. I have delightful living quarters in the graduate dormitory with a small living room, a private bath, and a little kitchenette, lots of closet space, and a very nice bedroom.

The academic load is terrific, but on top of that, being the only woman imposes quite a few extra demands. This morning, I had an appointment with the President of Radcliffe, Mrs. Mary Bunting, regarding educational programs for women in business. It is rumored that I am going to be invited to be on the White House Committee to Study the Status of Women. So I am taking every opportunity to expand my knowledge of the field in any way I can. Every night, I have tea with the famous British economist, Barbara Jackson. Tomorrow night, I'm taking the six girls in the Graduate Business School to dinner and having the 130 men in my program here for coffee at the Radcliffe Graduate Center after dinner.

Stephen is getting along wonderfully well, got all "A"s this report card and is really being co-operative. I think it is good for him. I called home tonight and…Helen assured me the boys are being very good. I go home for spring break the weekend of March 16, and I'm really looking forward to it…

Love, Peggy.

The Harvard program brought together top-level people in business and management for a 13-week period of recycling, and it was really tough—ten hours a day in class, five days a week, half-days on Saturdays. As the first woman to be admitted, at 39 I faced for the first time the full force of male chauvinism. I failed to mention in my letter home that the comfortable apartment across the river with the "Cliffies" was located as far as it could be from my classmates in Hamilton Hall. Their living arrangements were typically male apartments: four rooms, with two men in each room, grouped around a common bathroom facility. (I had no more desire to share the bathroom facilities with the men, than they had with me!) But I wondered why everyone else had the answers to the problems I struggled with late into the night? For the first time in my life, I was afraid I might fail. There were long telephone calls home, and I began to wonder, what am I doing here? When mid-semester break came in March, I packed my bags for a weekend in Washington and considered that I might not return.

But fate stepped in again. The morning before I left, one of my classmates—the only friend who had taken my side in the classroom debates—broke the ice and suggested that I might want to get to the Yard early the next morning. He was meeting the group for a working breakfast. I got up a half-hour earlier than usual and trudged across. When I sat down with my classmates over the coffee cups, I discovered why everyone else had the answers: the men handed out assignments every night, each one did the homework in his own specialty, then pooled the answers with the other guys in a team effort. I had been excluded from the system. Thereafter, I made sure I was at the Yard every morning in time for breakfast!

I was never able to win over some of the stuffy conservative sons of the Eastern Establishment, but I soon had a loyal coterie of friends among the young Texans and Californians who were leaders of new industries—Texas Instruments, Hewlett-Packard, Aerojet, and Xerox—who adopted me and gave me tips on their stocks. (The earlier trip to California had opened my eyes to the opportunities of developing high-tech growth stocks in Silicon Valley.)

One weekend, Jane Prentice and a friend from the office flew up to Boston to visit. She went to class with me on Saturday morning, and in the afternoon, joined an expedition of my Harvard group to the St. Lawrence Seaway in two chartered planes. We toured the facility and had lunch, then flew back to Boston. On Sunday morning, the two of us "toured" the men's dormitory. Jane remarked how these high-powered captains of industry lived in messy, ill-kept digs, without wives, maids, or "significant others" to care for their needs!

The Harvard program was a major turning point in my life. I went home to Washington for the break, determined to stick it out. After 13 weeks with 130 men, all top achievers in their chosen fields, I learned something valuable from the experience—I was as good as any of them, once I learned their system. I also discovered that the men had as many problems as I did.

Many of my classmates deeply resented the fact that a woman was in the group, and they made no bones about it. They thought I was there just to prove a point, until they realized I was a widow and the sole breadwinner for a family of six. The day of graduation, 11-year-old Stephen went with me to the reception. He was drinking a glass of fruit punch, when one of my classmates approached us and bumped his arm, causing the boy to spill punch down the front of his shirt. My friend apologized and took Stephen aside with an offer to clean him up. Later that evening, he told me he had bumped into Stephen on purpose to observe how he reacted. He thought children of women who were away from home at work for long hours must be emotionally insecure, and he was surprised to find my boy so well-adjusted. (It was hard for me to believe that story.)

I returned home from Harvard with renewed confidence. I decided to go for broke. Helen and I agreed to keep a small nest egg in the bank for emergencies, and to invest the rest in stocks. I reasoned if I lose, it isn't that much. But if I have a couple of winners, I might make enough to live really well. The long shots I invested in were the companies of my Harvard friends—Texas Instruments, Hewlett-Packard, Aerojet, and Xerox. In 18 months we quadrupled our nest egg.

The Harvard Business School experience was intended to put me on the advanced management track at Ferris & Company, but after a few weeks, I wanted to be back in production where I could be more creative *and* make more money. I used my public relations skills to win new clients.

Julia teaching an investment seminar at YWCA in Washington.

I was out front, lecturing to women's groups, the Army and Navy and Foreign Service Officers' wives. I went to parties and mingled, became active in community organizations.

I was invited to appear on "Inga's Angle," a daytime talk show for women on the local affiliate of NBC-TV. My friend Inga Hook thought my tips on the market would be helpful to other women. Mark, the youngest boy, sometimes went along to turn the flip-sheets for me. He became accustomed to seeing his mother on the TV screen at an early age.

My success in picking stocks began to attract attention from a large number of small investors. If this perfectly ordinary woman could do it, they asked, why can't I? By word of mouth, my name recognition spread. Only five short years after I became a widow, I was the highest income-earning woman in Washington, with a five-figure salary. Newscaster Sander Vanocur, Bud Wilkinson, the Oklahoma football coach turned business tycoon, Bob Linowes, diplomat and former president of the Board of Trade, chief arms negotiator General Edward Rowney, Admiral Elmo Zumwalt, Congressman Birch Bayh, and Ambassador Hugh Douglas were among my new clients. Though I was proud of such clients, those who pleased me most were widows with small accounts. Making a few dollars profit meant so much more to them, and I knew what it was like to walk in their shoes. I used the experience of my own personal tragedy to help them fight their way back, too.

Julia and Thomas Walsh on their wedding day, with Mary and Bill O'Connor, matron-of-honor and best man.

CHAPTER FIVE

A Good Merger and A Joint Venture

FOR SIX YEARS after John Montgomery's death, I never thought of remarrying. I concentrated on my job, and there was no lack of incentive. With six people to feed, there was not much time for more than superficial friendships.

To be sure, there were special male friends. Joe Cusco, the Georgetown coach, took the older boys to basketball games and often substituted in the father role. Several others bought gifts for the boys and took me out to dinner. George Ferris, Jr., kept in touch with letters while I was at Harvard, and urged me to hurry home, not just for business. We were seen together at dinner parties, and local gossips speculated whether we planned to become "partners" in personal as well as professional life.

After the Harvard experience, with 130 male classmates, I began to realize there were men out there who shared the same interests and family values. John Swain, a courtly, elegant San Francisco lawyer, came to Washington often on business, and for a time I considered him the love of my life. Not all were as distinguished and dapper as John. The boys still tease me about the unconventional Raul Giorgu, a Rumanian who drove a Nash Rambler and lived in a bachelor apartment across the Potomac in the Arlington Towers. As long as that friendship lasted, we had front row seats to watch the fireworks every Fourth of July.

There were very few who considered a permanent relationship with a widowed mother of four growing kids. My friend of long-standing and one-time beau, Mac MacCormac, was still waiting in the wings. But even if he had felt up to the job of being step-father to four growing boys, he was a Foreign Service Officer. I couldn't see my way clear to uproot our little family again and leave my very profitable job for an uncertain future in Bangkok. Bill O'Connor, a widower with several children of his own, was considerate and attentive, but he never mentioned merging. We remained good friends (and several years later, Bill was best man at my second wedding).

I realized it was time to start looking for another partner, if I didn't want to spend the rest of my life alone. I got a lot of help from matchmakers. I bought the Millwood Lane house from Bernard Long, a valued friend who helped me to network in the D.C. business community. Bernie gave a party to welcome me to the neighborhood. One of the guests was Thomas Walsh, a local business leader and president of Thomas D. Walsh, Inc., a real estate management company founded by his father. Tom came to the party alone because his wife was ill. We enjoyed each other's company that evening, but I ruled out seeing him again. He was a married man.

Sometime after that, Dr. Bill Faust, a neighbor on Lowell Lane and godfather of Tom Walsh's son Dan, invited us both to another party. When it was time to walk the short distance home after dark, Tom volunteered to escort me. Sometime later he called to ask me out to dinner, but I turned him down. I didn't know his wife had died that summer after a long illness. When I discovered he was a widower, I could offer true understanding—I had been there myself. Tom, too, was a devout Catholic. As we became closer friends, we discovered we both liked children. The fact that I was the mother of four boys didn't bother Tom: he had seven children of his own! If we merged, there would be a total of eleven kids between us. With the best intentions in the world, could we make it work?

I wanted to be married in the Church. And we were, on May 18, 1963, at St. John's Church in Clinton, Maryland. Tom's brother, Monsignor Francis Walsh, officiated. My friend Bill O'Connor and his wife Mary (the attractive widow and mother of seven who merged families with Bill's four), were best man and matron-of-honor. Only the older children were there—Tom's Mary, Kathleen, Joan, Tommy, and Patrick Joseph ("P.J."), and my Stephen and John. Kate Curry came from Ohio to see her daughter walk down the aisle, though it saddened both of us that my father, who died in 1962, was not there to witness our happiness. After the wedding, Tom and I slipped away for a quiet honeymoon in Hawaii. We stopped over at the Colony Surf near Kapiolani Park in Honolulu, then rented a cottage by the ocean in Lahaina, the old whaling village on the island of Maui. I came home relaxed and able to face the daunting tasks ahead, with a healthy tan and a colorful muumuu for summer parties tucked into my suitcase.

Tom Walsh and five of his seven children moved into the Millwood Lane house. P.J. was at Salem College in West Virginia most of the year, and Tom's oldest daughter, Mary, soon married Lieutenant (junior-grade) Steven Ferencie of the U.S. Navy. Our combined family consisted of two 6-year-olds (Anne and Mark), two 8-year-olds (Dan and Mike), two 11-year-olds (Joan and Stephen), one 13-year-old (John), one 15-year-old (Tom D.), and one 17-year-old Kathleen ("Kate"). The first summer, "the teenagers" (as they are still known within the family) were shipped down to Rehoboth Beach to sort out their situation, and miracle of miracles, it worked!

A Good Merger and A Joint Venture

We provided Helen Montgomery with a generous pension and an apartment near enough to visit us often. The Walsh and Montgomery "little kids" lunched almost daily at Helen's apartment, which was across the street from their grade school. She continued to be an important presence in our lives and to fill in when necessary until her death in 1969.

Grandmother Curry was also a frequent visitor to Millwood Lane. In later years, she came for Thanksgiving and stretched her visit through May, then returned to the family home in Akron, determined to retain her independence. A survivor of the Great Depression, Mother was a strict disciplinarian who didn't approve of the many gifts and advantages "the teenagers" took for granted. They teased her unmercifully, and to her dying day, my mother complained that the kids were spoiled and didn't work as hard for their many blessings as my brother and I did when we were growing up. A strong-minded woman, she bickered with Tom Walsh on many subjects— child-raising, politics, and the weather —arguments that ended amicably. They remained very good friends until her death in 1985.

We had to use all of the management skills and techniques I learned in my business career with the new family. For meals, I divided the children into two shifts. The younger ones (still known within the family as "the little kids") reported for breakfast at 7 o'clock. The older ones followed at 7:30, and got to school on their own, while we drove the younger ones. At dinner, the little kids ate first in the kitchen at 6:30; the rest of us gathered in the dining room an hour later.

Ours was a household where everyone shared the load, one advantage with such a large group. The children had their own built-in buddy and support system. Fortunately, in a two-career family we could afford additional household help. Our housekeeper Inez stayed from breakfast until two o'clock, her replacement came in at one o'clock, overlapped an hour, and stayed through dinner. During those early days there were sometimes ten to twelve people at home for the evening meal.

The next year, Kathleen started freshman year at Trinity College in Washington; the following year, Tommy enrolled at Georgetown University. John followed Tommy to Gonzaga High School. Stephen was at Georgetown Prep, later followed by Michael and Mark. Joan followed Kate to Immaculata. This was during the 70s, the time of the Vietnam War, so you can imagine what heated "discussions" took place around the table every night!

All of the children were taught something about the stock market. They heard about it at dinner, and some took business courses in school. We bought them stock early, and let them manage it in hands-on learning experiences. The first Christmas together, each child was given shares of stock in something he or she was interested in—Disney, for one example. Then, if someone wanted a bicycle, he or she had to sell a few shares of stock to buy it.

To make an even dozen, one year after our marriage, Margaret Elizabeth ("Peggy, Jr."), my only daughter, was born. She became known as the "joint venture," and later referred to herself as the only one *really* related to everyone else! She admits to being spoiled, growing up as the baby girl among so many boys. There were some conflicts with Tom's two middle daughters, Joan and Kate, and the years from 12 to 16 were difficult. I'm sure both girls wished they had a mother that stayed at home, even though a substitute was always on hand for school activities. (By the time Peggy was in school, her father was nearing retirement age and available to fill in when I couldn't get away.)

The kids laugh now about the transition period, when we were trying to become one family. There were some really rough times, though I tried to deal with the crises in a rational, problem-solving way. I wanted to give each child an equal measure of time, but in emergencies, when someone needed extra TLC, I made an exception. Even then, with my busy life, the young people sometimes had to make an appointment to see me.

This was not easy for 11-year-old Joan, entering her 'teens. Five years into the marriage, when she was a senior at Immaculata Preparatory School, I was invited to attend Ring Day, a Mother/Daughter day of Mass and luncheon just before graduation, one of the biggest events of the year. Perhaps out of rebellion, or a fleeting frugality, she was one of only four girls in the class who decided not to buy a ring. There was a conflict in my schedule, since I was to appear on local television on the noon-time interview show, "Panorama," on Ring Day. When Joan reported to the Sister in charge that her mother wouldn't be there, the Sister exploded: "I don't care *who* your mother is, she should be there!" Joan replied, "My mother has better things to do than to watch me *not* get a ring!"

That evening, Sister called me to report the exchange. I replied, "Thank you for telling me, Sister. You have let me know that Joan understands, at last, what I'm all about!" Joan recognized that I was a different kind of mother, that I *cared*, though I didn't stay home to bake cookies and drive the carpool. I must have been a positive role model. Later Joan graduated from the Master's Weekend Program at Wharton, and then she took a challenging position at the National Petroleum Council and was elected president of the American News Women's Club.

There were times when two or more of "the teen-agers" were going to different places on the same night and each one needed a car. We established the honor system, with a curfew of 11 o'clock. When one of the girls came home late, and one of the boys told on her, what a ruckus followed! Generally, the boys covered for one another (they were in trouble a lot more often than the girls). The "help" usually seemed to favor the boys, perhaps because the boys developed better political skills?

I was lucky to find the right man in Tom Walsh, himself an understanding father. Both of us had lived long enough to acquire maturity and perspective on difficult situations, and we went into the marriage determined to stick with it. The idea that if it didn't work, we'd just quit, never entered our minds. You couldn't put that group together with anything but a permanent commitment.

II

At times, the Millwood Lane house seemed to be exploding at the seams. The house at Rehoboth Beach we owned early in the marriage proved too far from Washington for a weekend retreat. We began to look for another real estate investment, one where we could get away from the demands of our busy lives. In 1969, we finally settled on the hunt country near Middleburg, Virginia, an hour's drive from Washington.

Our first place at Round Hill was a traditional house on the main road in the heart of town. We settled there for a year-and-a-half, but with such a large family, we soon needed to expand. When we moved to a farm farther out, we hoped we were getting farther away from the telephone. But our friends and the children's friends, and friends of friends, got our number, so it was seldom quiet. We named it "Walmont," after the merged Walsh and Montgomery families.

Some of our well-to-do neighbors up the road apiece were Joe Allbritton, later president of Riggs Bank, and Jack Kent Cooke, owner of the Redskins. Allbritton fit right in, as a noted horse breeder, but Cooke got off to a bad start because he missed the Orange County hunt breakfast—it was considered an honor to be invited. The point-to-point races were the most popular form of entertainment, and without owning horses, we were afraid we might face discrimination.

A Good Merger and A Joint Venture

Middleburgers are notorious for turning their noses up at those who don't ride to the hounds or don't let the hunt pass over their property.

It wasn't long before we bought "Lady," an easy-going mare for the whole family. Later, we added "Strawberry," Mark's horse, "Bay Rum" for Michael, and another for Anne. After we got the horses, we had to invest in a large double-horse van. Kate didn't take to the saddle, but she was a good driver, and every weekend in the fall and spring she would load riders and horses into the van and take them to Winchester or the nearest point-to-point race.

Peggy was still a toddler when we started going to the country on weekends, but she loved to tag along with Mike, Mark and Anne, and later became a good rider. The first Christmas Peggy was old enough to sit a horse, "Santa Claus" delivered a Chincoteague pony in the back seat of a station wagon to the house on Millwood Lane! (Stephen and Joan had been to France that summer, and they brought back a rabbit-fur coat for "Princess Peggy," who wore it proudly with a little black velvet Chanel-type suit.)

Christmas in July was a tradition at Walmont. I always started my shopping a year ahead. When I saw something I knew one of the young people would like, I tucked it away in my shopping bag and didn't wait for December. I always saved my "L'Eggs" (egg-shaped) stocking containers to hang on the tree stuffed with half-dollars.

Then there were the dogs. First, came Mark's sheltie, "Angus," which could always be seen in the back seat of the car when we drove around the countryside. (He was Helen Montgomery's dog until she died, when we had to adopt him.) Next came a sky terrier named "Bonnie." With so much land for the animals to roam in, the kids would not be satisfied until we acquired "Clyde," the St. Bernard (the other half of "Bonnie and Clyde"). We thought Clyde would be happy at Walmont, but soon he was caught red-handed poaching on the neighbors' sheep, so we had to ship him off to a friend's ranch in Texas.

Even non-equestrian members of the family enjoyed those country weekends, and they brought their friends with them. Amy Williams, our good-natured Trinidad cook who has been with the family for 30 years, remembers putting 20 or more pieces of chicken on the stone grill for almost any family dinner, plus some three- or four-dozen ears of freshly-shucked corn, and several gallons of potato salad for the assembled clan. She really believed in "the more the merrier," and was never happier than when we had a raging pool party going on. (Many weekends there were as many as 50.) We were a bit surprised when a Communist magazine from Moscow came to write about us and to take photos of our capitalist establishment and neighbors!

It was easier to own these properties in the late 1970s and early 1980s than it is today, because of the tax advantages. Our vacation homes were an early lesson in tax-sheltered investments. We were sorry when we had to sell out during the lean times that followed, but though we owned Walmont for only five good years, we never regretted buying it.

⚜III

The decade of the 70s was a time of family weddings. One of our children was already established in a home of her own. Mary Walsh and Steven Ferencie were married in 1964, the year after our marriage, at Our Lady of Victory Church on MacArthur Boulevard.

Over the Easter holidays in 1969, the Walshes—Kate, Dan, other members of the extended family and "Aunt Elizabeth" Borne—flew to Bonaire for the wedding of Tom D. Walsh and his fianceé, Patricia Brandon, then an employee of D.C. National Bank. Monsignor Walsh officiated at the mass at high noon in the old stone (Catholic) church, and Peggy, Jr., then three-years-old, wore her favorite pink-linen dress when she led the procession down the aisle as flower girl. (She was disappointed not to be invited on the honeymoon!) A civil ceremony followed, after which Pat's parents hosted a reception at a beautiful island hotel. Patrick Joseph (P.J.) and Kathy Walsh were married in July 1970.

Stephen and his beautiful Elizabeth (Beth) Koehler were next. During the 70s, my stepdaughter Kate shared a house on Q Street in Georgetown with Stephen (another of my real estate investments). All of the children invited their friends to the Georgetown house for great parties. Beth's roommate had a blind date with John to a Redskins' game, and later John introduced Beth to Stephen. Mac MacCormac was home on leave that summer, and Beth prepared a delicious Thai dinner for the Q Street-house gang. Stephen planned to return with Mac to Thailand, but he never made it. He fell in love with Beth and didn't want to lose her to someone else while he was gone. They were married on New Years' Eve 1979 in the Jesuit Church of the Holy Trinity in Georgetown, then flew to Paris on their honeymoon (more about that later).

When my administrative assistant Jane Wyman, who was almost "family," was married in June 1977, I offered the garden of the Millwood Lane house to her mother for the reception. In October of the same year, Joan Walsh married Brian Cassedy in Trinity Church, Georgetown.

My son John Montgomery and Maryann Pflepsen were married in September 1978 in the Dalgren Chapel of Georgetown University where John was, and still is, on the adjunct faculty. The reception was at the Millwood Lane house afterwards. Maryann's wedding ring, which had been Helen Montgomery's, was the one her son John gave to me on our wedding day some 30 years before. It was a sentimental moment when John placed it on Maryann's finger. Maryann was (and still is) a flight attendant, so they took advantage of her passes to travel to the Far East on their honeymoon. They visited our devoted family friend, Kenneth MacCormac, in Bangkok. Mac was retired from the Foreign Service and serving as a consultant with the U.S. Educational (Fulbright) Commission.

The last of "the teen-agers" were married in the 80s. Kathleen (Kate) Walsh and Keith Armistead Carr exchanged vows in June 1980. Anne Walsh and Robert G. Walton were next; they were married at Our Lady of Victory Church in September. In April 1988, Daniel and Helene Walsh's wedding at St. Joseph's Church on Capitol Hill was followed by a lovely reception at the Capitol Hill Club.

A time of family weddings: the Walshes on Anne's big day.

By the 1980s, Tom and I had recouped our losses and bought another vacation home in the Blue Ridge Mountains near the Gettysburg Gap in Pennsylvania. (This was the historic passage through which General Lee escaped after the famous battle, with the Union troops hot in pursuit.) We shared "Far and Near" with John and his wife Maryann, and Joan and her husband Brian Cassedy and the grandchildren. Kate and Keith rented a small cottage nearby.

Life has been good to the Walshes. Our merger was a positive investment in the future. Finally after 35 years we sold Millwood Lane and moved to an apartment at Watson Place in the same neighborhood. Against all odds, Tom and I are still together, as happy as any two people can be, subject to the headaches and heartaches, as well as the joys, of the previous 30 years.

The Montgomery-Walsh clan, from left front: Andrew Montgomery, Tom Carr, Kathleen Walsh, Keith Carr, Tom Walton, Trisha Walsh, Julia Montgomery, Julia Montgomery Walsh, Claire Walton, Tom Walsh, Kate Walsh Carr, Carolyn Cassedy, Pat Walsh, Anne Walsh Walton, Steven Montgomery, Helene Walsh, Mary Walsh, Maryann Montgomery, John Montgomery, "Buck" Montgomery Jr.; standing: Tom D. Walsh, P.J. Walsh, Joan Cassedy, Kirsten Walsh, Amy Williams, Dan Walsh, Kerry Walsh, Bob Walton, Steven Ferencie, Anne Walton, Beth Montgomery, Keith Carr, Kathy Walsh, George Montgomery, Brian Cassedy, Joan Cassedy, Peggy Cornog, Rob Cornog, Michael Montgomery, Mark Montgomery.

Julia—more at home in the stock market than in the supermarket.

CHAPTER SIX

Having It All—A Woman In The New Era

IN THE DECADE of my 40s, all the pieces of my
life seemed to fit. The merged household was, for me, "having
it all." In 1965, women were gaining recognition in many
formerly male-dominated fields. One year after our daughter,
Peggy Jr., was born at Georgetown Hospital, I achieved
another "first." Phyllis S. Peterson, a colleague from Sade &
Company, another Washington brokerage, and I applied
to the admissions committee for seats on the American Stock
Exchange. There was nothing in the regulations of either
of the two major stock exchanges to bar women from joining.
Several women were already associate members, being general
partners in brokerage firms that were members of an exchange.
But ours were the first applications before the committee from
women who wanted to become *full* members and own seats in
their own names. Both of us met the qualifications—we had
been in the securities business for more than six months, we
were American citizens, we met the exchange requirements for
health, character, and financial standing. There was no legal
reason why we should not apply. They could not turn us down.

When the 32 members of the Board of Governors of AMEX met in November 1965, they voted to break with a 116-year-old tradition by admitting two *women*. The business and financial section of *The New York Times* featured stories about this groundbreaking decision. Phyllis Peterson and Julia Montgomery Walsh were the first to gain seats on either of the nation's two largest exchanges.

I was beginning to gain national as well as local recognition as a pioneer woman in the investment industry. In 1966, a *Time* magazine article reported my success as the "Highest Paid Woman in Business," with a six-figure salary.

Lyndon Baines Johnson had been elected President of the U.S. in 1964, and as a lifelong Democrat, I was pleased to do my share for the Party when asked to serve with Treasurer Larry O'Brien of the Democratic National Committee in 1966. Senator Margaret Chase Smith saw to it that I was invited to a reception at the White House, my first since the college visit with Eleanor Roosevelt. Everyone who has met "LBJ" will agree that he was a strong personality who used his charm and folksy manner to win friends and influence people. I was no exception. And the President was no less charismatic than his wife Lady Bird, who could charm the wings off a butterfly!

I was also asked to sponsor many Washington charities. "Project Hope" was one of them. William B. Walsh, M.D. (no relation), who served as medical officer aboard a Navy destroyer in the South Pacific during World War II, was so moved by the poor health conditions in that area that he envisioned a floating medical center that would bring improved care to underdeveloped communities around the world. In 1958, while a member of the President's People-to-People initiatives, Dr. Walsh persuaded President Eisenhower to donate a U.S. Navy hospital ship to serve in this peacetime mission. With only $150, a dream and the support of American industry, the ship was transformed into the S.S. *Hope*.

The Walshes attended the 1968 Hope Ball at the Washington Hilton Hotel, with Admiral Elmo Zumwalt who headed the Asian fleet in Vietnam, and other VIPS as major contributors. When Mrs. Emil Mosbacher, Jr., a member of the board of "Project Hope" and various other health-care organizations, organized a cruise as a fund-raiser, Tom and I took time out from our busy schedules for a second honeymoon in the Caribbean. Most of the family went to New York for a bon voyage party to see us off. We looked very tan and jolly in a group picture at Half Moon Bay in Jamaica with our friends Murray and Grace Toomey and other fellow passengers.

That summer, I went back to Rome again with the "little kids," Michael, Mark and Anne (who were not so little now). We stayed at the Hassler Hotel as a guest of my old friend from the Foreign Service, Carmen Wirth. Carmen married the Swiss hotelier who then owned the Hassler, and she always treated us royally whenever I returned to Rome.

On the same trip, I visited Thomas Duffy, the General Electric representative in Iran, for an "insider's" tour of that country during the glory days of Reza Shah Pahlevi. I had attended several of the glamorous parties at the Embassy residence on Massachusetts Avenue near the Mosque in Washington when Adeshir Zahedi was Ambassador, and I was curious to see that opulent city. Teheran was the site of the famous World War II conference in 1943 when Roosevelt, Churchill and Stalin made plans for the invasion of France. The narrow streets were broadened and large, contemporary buildings were erected on the site of the old town during the reign of Shah Pahlevi. I was awestruck by the opulent Peacock Throne and the royal treasury of crown jewels brought back after the invasions of India in the 1700s. Tom Duffy also drove us to the ancient burial ground of the Shahs' ancestors.

Another idyllic time mixing business and pleasure was at beautiful Lake Chatauqua. The Chatauqua Institute of New

Julia at the White House with President Lyndon Baines Johnson:
Two strong personalities discuss the nation's economy.

York asked me to do a series of lectures on investment for some 300 bright young entrepreneurs. Tom and I took Anne and Mark with us and put them in day camp. After hours and on weekends, the family went swimming and sailing on the lake. I thought at the time that heaven must be very much like this.

In 1971, I was the first woman to address a meeting of the D.C. Bankers' Association, at "The Greenbriar" in White Sulphur Springs, West Virginia. (At that time, I was a member of the advisory board of the First National Bank of Washington.) To the large audience, primarily male, I offered one bit of advice from my own experience: if men intend to understand the buying habits of the American people, they must first recognize that *women* are CEOs of the most important economic unit of all, the family! Traditionally, while men were making money, women made the major decisions about how to allocate the family resources, what portion to spend and how much to save. Women decided when and where to make the major purchases. With more women in the workplace today, they are controlling the purse strings in the majority of American homes.

Our boys were growing up—P.J. Walsh graduated from Georgetown Prep in '62, Stephen would finish in '69, Mark and Michael in the 70s. I was asked to serve for six years on the Board of Trustees and to help Father Vincent Beatty establish the school's endowment fund. He came to my office one day with a file folder full of stock certificates that were donated to Prep and asked me what to do with them.

At that time, smaller institutions had no formal investment committees or policies, and even some larger ones had very little. Stocks were considered a risky investment. People who had lived through the Great Depression, and even those who had just heard stories were vicariously gun-shy. In my view, the stock market always has been "the only game in town." Father

Beatty and I agreed that being fearful was simply impractical. We couldn't afford *not* to invest in stocks.

One of the first stocks Prep owned was Atlantic Richfield. Someone donated it to the school, but many people considered that energy stocks had no value at the time. I insisted that Prep hold onto the Atlantic stock, which increased in value from $20,000 to $200,000 before we converted it to another successful investment. Father Beatty and I found ourselves with the makings of a wonderful endowment program, by the grace of God and some great gifts!

While most of the family spent the summer of 1972 at Walmont, I rushed off to New York to attend meetings of the ASE, then flew to Tunisia with my husband, who wanted to visit the World War II battlefields. Tom and I checked into the Hilton Hotel in Tunis, and soon after we arrived, a brother of the Tunisian Ambassador to the U.S. whisked us away on a personally conducted sightseeing tour. German General Rommel, the "Desert Fox," had set up defenses along the Mareth Line, a former French bastion, when Allied troops under the Supreme Command of General Dwight D. Eisenhower engaged in bitter fighting in the Tunisian hills. They suffered heavy losses in the region of the Faid and Kassarine Passes, before the Axis finally capitulated in May 1943.

The Summer Olympics were underway when I arrived in Munich. My 24-year-old son John, then backpacking in Greece, and Kenneth MacCormac met me there. I was invited to stay with Erne Brucher, my old friend from the Foreign Service. Erne had changed very little in some 20 years, but I was pleased to see that there were many improvements in the post-war city. We could ride the subway instead of the antiquated trolley line that used to run the length of the Ludwigstrasse!

On that trip, our family was traveling in high circles. After I left Munich in the mid-40s, Mac MacCormac stayed on

Having It All—A Woman In The New Era

for some ten years as Cultural Attaché. He cultivated the friendship of Max von Bayern, pretender to the throne of Bavaria, and his two sisters, Eleanora and Dorothea. Max was a grandson of the brother that deposed "Mad" King Ludwig, a great-grandson of Franz Joseph and Maria Theresa of Austria. He is now a gentleman farmer with a large estate on Lake Starnberger, south of Munich.

Mac arranged for John and himself to stay with the would-be King and Queen. John reported that he was impressed by the row-upon-row of ancestor portraits on the walls of the stately mansion, and that when he walked through the village with the von Bayerns, the townspeople bowed and scraped as they passed by. They treated all of us to royal hospitality, and it was a summer to remember. We were especially proud when Mark Spitzer of the U.S. team won seven gold medals in swimming at the Olympics! We fortunately departed Munich the morning that the Palestinian terrorists captured Israeli athletes and held them hostage. We managed to leave with only good memories and headed south for another stay at the Hotel Hassler in Rome.

On this same bittersweet nostalgia trip, my son John and I went back to the house on the hill in Ankara where we had once lived. We had not seen it since our departure in 1955 and now found it occupied by the Turkish office of EXXON.

One cold February day in 1972, I came home to find a florist's truck blocking the driveway. When I stepped into the house, I thought I'd died and gone to heaven. There were so many flowers it looked like a coffin should be placed in the middle! My friends on Wall Street were acknowledging that I had really made it. Seven years after becoming a member of the American Stock Exchange, I was nominated for membership on the 33-member AMEX Board of Governors. The nomination, tantamount to election on April 10, meant that I would be only the second woman—the *first* from the securities industry—to serve on the board of a major stock exchange. A color photo on the wall of my office shows a dozen or so somber-faced gentlemen in banker's-gray suits, and there am I in the second row in back, wearing a gray dress, adopting the same pose. (I should have worn yellow or pink, so I'd stand out!) Chairman Arthur Levitt (now chairman of the Securities and Exchange Commission) was an early mentor of mine. He was very good about treating women on the board just like everyone else.

I was thrilled over my nomination but I knew, in part, that my good luck came because the time was right for a woman—it couldn't have happened even ten years before. The kids were excited about my new challenge, since they had visions of going back and forth to New York with me and having an exotic time.

So much was happening in the industry at that time, affecting the final direction of the Exchange, that I was delighted to have the opportunity to take part in making those decisions. The AMEX was dying on the vine: the small companies were listed on the NASDAQ, the majors on the Big Board. In the 70s, I would mark out a deal where I could find someone to do the other side of a trade and develop a market for a selected stock. It was this stock-option trading plan of "puts" and "calls" that put buyers and sellers together that helped AMEX to survive.

Also during the Nixon Administration, two years before Home Rule and the citizens of the District of Columbia won the right to vote in national elections, I was named to replace Lt. General Elwood P. Quesada (then retiring) on the board of the Pennsylvania Avenue Development Corporation (PADC). This was one of the most satisfying and challenging opportunities of my life.

The movement to widen and improve the Avenue had its roots during the Administration of John F. Kennedy, when the new President remarked on the ugly buildings along the route of the Inaugural parade in the nation's capital.

One of our first projects was the renovation of the Old Post Office Building with a series of trendy shops and restaurants that brought new life to the inner city and saved another historic building from the wrecker's ball. The Willard Hotel, with a long history dating back to before the Civil War and Presidents Lincoln and Grant, was standing empty for many years while citizens' groups tried to decide what to do with it. Restored to its former beauty, it is again a favorite rendezvous for Washingtonians and visitors who use it for social occasions and business meetings.

John Hechinger, a Democrat and successful businessman, was an early activist for Home Rule on the City Council. Max N. Berry, a lawyer and fund raiser, and Joseph B. Danzansky, president of the Giant Food Company, also spearheaded the movement. After Home Rule was successfully established in 1974, the development of downtown Washington was phenomenal (some 24 million square feet of new office space). Tom and I were great friends of Walter Washington, D.C.'s first African American mayor since Reconstruction, who often visited our country place at Round Hill with Bud Doggett and other civic leaders.

☙ II

During this era, as I traveled around the U.S. (from Missouri to Texas to California) for business, I was beginning to notice the "volatility" of the national scene with protests against the Vietnam War. I was shocked and saddened in 1970 when I heard that four students had been shot by the National Guard at my alma mater, Kent State University. A few years later, there was an enormous amount of concern over President

Richard M. Nixon and the Watergate affair. The energy crisis was the real culprit to blame for declining stock prices of 1973 and 1974, and Watergate was not affecting the day-to-day market in any way analysts could measure, but attention was being focused on it. Small investors were becoming nervous and afraid.

Inflation was rising and economic growth was slowing on December 4, 1972, when Elizabeth MacDonald Manning, publisher of *Finance* magazine, invited me to moderate the third annual Bank Trust's Round Table. Manning, who operated *Finance* out of her mansion off Fifth Avenue, was a client, and my older sons, Stephen and John, both worked for her while attending New York University. (John received an MBA in Finance, and Stephen, a BA in Journalism, both in 1974.)

At the so-called "Hundred Billion Dollar Round Table" (the major Bank Trust departments represented assets well in excess of $100 billion, and were by far the dominating institutional investors of that era), most of the time was spent brainstorming solutions to the problems of the securities markets and regulations. There was a lot going on about the trials and tribulations of how to measure discretionary accounts vs. personal trusts vs. investment performance overall. What is now Morgan Guaranty was resting comfortably on its $26-billion trust assets, and it was clear that all New York City banks had set record performances in 1972.

The forum brought out banking's best and brightest, with an audience of former Young Presidents (all under the age of 49): Bank of America's Douglas Heidhorn, Lawrence Katzman, president of KAZ, Inc., Charles Johnston of Chase Manhattan Bank, and Charles George of Lee Myles. One after the other stood up to say one should own and continue to buy one of the "nifty fifty" growth stocks which had done so well in the late 1960s and early 1970s.

Having It All—A Woman In The New Era

I, and many others, were aware that most stocks had been languishing or declining in price since 1968, while the major market averages were going up with the prices of these large "one-decision" stocks. I reckoned that all the major institutional investors owned these companies already, and wondered how much more they should buy. Or more important, what would happen if these huge institutions decided to sell? I was uncomfortable with the gathering storm clouds on the economic and political horizon and went back to Washington determined to sell the Xeroxes, IBMs, Eastman Kodaks and Polaroids from my clients' portfolios. While most clients reluctantly agreed, many refused to sell these Wall Street darlings (especially given capital gains taxes). In 1973 and 1974, the one-decision stocks were taken out and shot. The major averages declined by 40 to 50 percent, while many stocks disappeared. There was blood on the Street.

My son John and I regularly attended the Securities Industry Association meetings in Boca Raton, Florida. These were grim confabs when industry leaders got together in 1973 and 1974 to discuss problems and opportunities, more of the former than the latter. On a cruise that took place afterwards, I remember one of my colleagues taking out his briefcase and emptying it, then he began throwing the papers wistfully, one by one, off the back of the boat, followed by the briefcase!

In the industry consolidation of 1968-70, securities firms had experienced enough good years to build up reserves. But by the mid-1970s, there was little fat to trim. Those were the grim years, when the market went to hell in a handbasket. In 1974, the Dow Jones industrial average fell below 600, the lowest level since the 1970 recession. The tax laws also changed. (That was the year we had to sell our country home, "Walmont," since our tax burden was greater than our income.) Ferris & Company also found it advantageous to convert from a partnership to a corporation, causing a year of double taxation liability for the former partners. We began to concentrate on long-term estate planning. I worked long days and into the night, trying to hold things together for our family and clients.

I was well rewarded for my labor. *Business Week* included me on their list of "100 Top Women Executives" throughout the U.S. During the same era, I was named "Business Woman of the Year" by the local Business and Professional Women's Club. I was equally proud to be honored as "Business and Professional Woman of the Year" by the Religious Heritage of America at the awards luncheon in the Washington Hilton Hotel.

At Christmas, our family was invited to go to Florida on the Auto Train in the posh private cars of the president and chairman of Amtrak. A special treat for the "little kids."

It was a very busy time in my life, but I was never too busy to adopt a cause I believe in, such as education for women. I went back to New England to take part in a symposium, "Women in Business," at Simmons College in 1974. The Simmons Business School program was developed by Professors Margaret Hennig and Anne Jardim, with whom I had networked while attending the Harvard Advanced Management Program. I worked hard to raise funds to set up the Business School program and served on their advisory board. It was exciting to see so many different age groups expressing interest in it. (I was tempted to enroll and work toward a Master's degree myself!) I was especially happy to meet older women who went to college before "liberation," as I did. It is the 30-and-over age group that has seen things turn around.

In my view, all-women colleges are under-credited for their role in developing the intellectual, individualistic, and active women of today our society needs. When a small Catholic college that our daughter Anne attended, St. Mary-of-the-Woods in Indiana, asked me to serve on its board, I was happy to do so. I also helped to set up their endowment fund.

In June of that year, I was elected vice-chairman of the Board of Ferris & Company. When I first went to work 20 years before as a novice sales person on commission with only a desk and a telephone but no salary, I had no idea I would ever achieve that position. I was pleased that two other women, Sally A. Behn and Gail Winslow, had the opportunity to follow in my footsteps as senior vice presidents.

Alexandra Armstrong began to learn the business as my administrative assistant. Alex later went on to become one of the first Certified Financial Planners as a pioneer in her own right in the financial planning profession. I was so busy I couldn't give new clients the time and attention they deserved. I started looking for someone else to back me up. My associate at Ferris, Gail Winslow, suggested Jane Wyman, a woman who had been working as office manager and registered representative for a national mutual fund company. Her organization closed its Washington office and left her without a job. In May 1974, Jane came to work at Ferris as my assistant and registered sales representative. I particularly liked the fact that she was *registered*, freeing me to attend board meetings and other activities without letting the business suffer.

We were always looking for new clients. With Jane's help, I initiated a series of seminars and lectures, usually held at the American News Women's Club or the International Club in downtown Washington, among the very few clubs (at that time) that admitted women. These seminars were well attended, and Jane would follow up by arranging appointments, answering questions, and sending out the requested literature. Her hard work, quality performance on the job, and proven loyalty for the past 20 years are indeed rare in today's work place.

Many of my early clients have become lifelong friends. I helped them to add to their portfolios and/or to start new careers. Jeanne Beekhuis, who now heads her own organization in tourism and real estate development, started by investing a small nest egg with Ferris & Company. One particularly hectic day, when we were going down in the elevator after an important meeting with corporate executives, she said, "Julia, I don't see how you manage it all, to keep tabs on the business with 12 young people at home. You're a miracle woman!" I shared my secret for coping with a large family such as ours: we sometimes raise our voices and disagree among ourselves, but it is absolutely *verboten* to speak sharply to our much-appreciated housekeeper. At home, *she's* the boss!

Another friend who learned the brokerage business from me was Beth Wainwright. She came to our firm with a small savings account to invest, and two little boys to raise on her own. I knew how hard it was for her, since I had walked in her shoes. In our early conversations, I discovered Beth had a real aptitude for the business. I suggested that she study the market and prepare to take the exam to qualify as a registered broker.

"But, Julia," she protested, "I've never mastered the multiplication tables. I was never good at math!" Like many young women, Beth was suffering from "math anxiety," and was never encouraged in school to excel in that field. I hope I gave her renewed confidence. A devout Catholic like myself, Beth said later that a Higher Power stepped in to help her answer those questions. She is still a valued member of the team at Julia Walsh & Sons/Tucker Anthony.

Another client who played an important role in our family life was Elizabeth Borne, fondly remembered as "Aunt Elizabeth" by the children. A single woman who lived in a modest house near Chevy Chase Circle with two elderly aunts, she first came to me desperately in need of extra income from her investments. After the aunts died, she had no other imme-

diate family, so she became a member of ours. She was at
Millwood Lane for many important family celebrations beginning with Mark's third birthday, thereafter for Thanksgiving
and Christmas dinners. When Elizabeth was stricken with a
major stroke at the Christmas dinner table in 1973, we were
there to arrange for her hospitalization. We continued to look
after her like a member of the family until her death in 1975.
(Our daughter Peggy bears the middle name of Elizabeth.)

❧III

In the mid-70s, I received a call from Fred Allen, then CEO of
Pitney Bowes, the major office machines company, asking me
to come to New York and meet him under the clock at the
Biltmore Hotel. I wondered why, but I went. I was interested
when he invited me to become a member of the board of
directors of that company. At that time, I was to be the first of
three women on their board. Pitney Bowes always had a good
record for moving women from staff to line jobs. (By August
1990, the cover of *Business Week* featured Pitney as one of the
top companies for women: then-CEO George Harvey
mandated that 35 percent of all professional hires and promo-
tions would go to women; 15 percent of the top managers were
women; two women were reporting directly to the CEO.)

Even in the early 90s, only a few women came to boards
from business; more came from academic fields. In the
past, there was a great deal of tokenism in major corporations;
women philanthropists were named to boards simply to "deco-
rate" them. An article in the *Los Angeles Times* in 1983 reported
that only 367 women were on the boards of directors of the
1,300 largest corporations in America!

When I first joined the board of Wayne-Gossard, a leader
in the field of women's undergarments, my male colleagues
paid no attention to me. Like many women of my era, I was
trained to listen, not to speak out. Later, when I joined the

board of Georgetown University, I spoke up when I thought it advantageous to buy a valuable property at 35th and Reservoir Road, and I lost that battle because no one listened. On the other hand, when Don Kelly, a real "wheeler and dealer," invited me to serve on the board of Esmark, the Chicago conglomerate, *he listened*. Don wanted my input and encouraged me to speak up, so I was able to make a real contribution. In the 90s, the number of women on corporate boards more than tripled, but the door is still only slightly ajar for minority women, and only 3 percent of the *inside* directors are women, those drawn from top management.

When I started to work, I had to succeed by my own talents and abilities, years before the "women's liberation" movement. The words "sex discrimination" weren't even in our vocabulary. The crusade for equal rights was making it easier for young women entering the work force than it had been for me. August 26, 1970, marked the 50th anniversary of women's winning the right to vote. The marches to commemorate that event brought "the movement" into national consciousness. In New York alone, 50,000 people turned out! Women by this time were considered a *majority*, not a radical minority.

In the early '70s, the movement was just getting off the ground when Margaret Henning and Anne Jardim, founders of the Simmons Business School program, suggested my meeting with Betty Friedan, founder of the National Organization for Women (NOW) and author of the groundbreaking book, *The Feminine Mystique* (1963). Young Gloria Steinem, publisher of *Ms.* magazine, was also among the women they contacted.

At that time, when I had business meetings in New York, I shared a penthouse apartment on the Upper East Side with my sons John, attending New York University Graduate Business School, and Stephen, an undergraduate at NYU. (I cannot help mentioning how different my education had been from theirs, and how my early days in New York as a wage slave for W.R. Grace differed from their lifestyle at the same age. Instead of spaghetti restaurants in the Village, my adult sons went around the corner to the Cafe Carlyle to listen to Bobby Short.)

John was the only male present when I invited Friedan and Steinem and other leaders of the movement to a brain-storming session at the apartment to exchange ideas. Muriel Siebert, the first woman on the East Coast to own a brokerage firm and former Commissioner of Banking for the State of New York, was also in the group.

After the battle for women's suffrage in the 20s, the crusade for women's rights went nowhere through the 50s. In the 70s, we were trying to make up for lost time. At this meeting, we discussed such issues as equal pay for women. (It seemed obvious to us that the school teacher and nurse should be paid at least as much as the truck driver and the garbage collector.) With women entering the work force in greater numbers, we talked about the need for men to share the burdens of child rearing and the restructuring of institutions to allow for maternity and paternity leave and "flextime." We also took note of the burgeoning divorce rate, a sign of women's newly-won economic independence. On the plus side, the couples who stay together do so for the *right* reasons, not because they have to. Most of us agreed that there will always be a need for the home, for commitment, and intimacy.

I was pleased to know that among Ms. Friedan's most-admired American women was my idol, Eleanor Roosevelt. She also mentioned Margaret Mead as a role model, and Abigail Adams, the wife of the second President. Madame de Staël, the French diarist and novelist, was—in Friedan's view— an early example of the woman who "had it all." She would nurse a baby, select a menu for the cook, wave goodbye to a lover going off to the Napoleonic wars—all the while writing extraordinary stories and novels. While I cannot remember any memorable sayings of Ms. Steinem, her presence was a positive force. She was wearing her signature dark glasses, a T-shirt, and blue-jeans held together with an unusual belt contrived from cat collars!

The year 1975 marked the United Nations International Women's Year (IWY), the beginning of the U.N. Decade for Women. Back in Washington Dorothy B. Ferebee, a medical doctor and chair of the local IWY Committee, founded the Women's Institute, a non-lobbying, non-profit organization and a vital catalyst for programming on issues of major concern to women.

I was asked to serve as treasurer, Meg Connor as executive vice president, secretary and executive director, and June Carter Perry as first vice president. Esther Lawton and Rita Z. Johnston were named to the executive committee. We began by working with key leadership in government and industry.

The Institute's goal was to educate and train women to give them greater career choices, utilizing the resources of the metropolitan Washington area. We joined the American University in offering a "Styles for Leadership" lecture series, designed to reach both academic and non-academic audiences.

The Institute soon gained visibility on the local and national scenes and a reputation for promoting innovative model programs. Among other on-going projects was the Women's Institute Press, the Myra E. Barrer Special Library Collection on Women (housed in the Bender Library at American University) and the Barrer Journalism award, and a collection on Black Women Physicians housed at the Medical College of Pennsylvania in memory of its founding president, Dorothy Ferebee. The Institute also started its national conferences for college women, student leaders and other women of distinction.

Having It All—A Woman In The New Era

Beginning in 1979, the Institute presented the United Nations Human Rights Award to a distinguished woman at the annual luncheon. I was unable to attend the 20th Anniversary celebration because of my health, but I was pleased to receive a "certificate of recognition" in appreciation of my role as a founding member.

Another highlight of the 1970s was an invitation to join the panel of financial experts on "Wall $treet Week With Louis Rukeyser," Maryland Public Television's attempt to make the stock market and economics understandable to the layman. From its inception in November 1970, I watched the program with extra interest. Lou's informal approach and easy banter soon won an estimated audience of millions of viewers nationwide, and it is still one of the most popular shows on PBS.

I was the only woman and one of about two-dozen regulars who appeared on a rotating basis with a "special guest" to trade information about the market and make predictions. The show was taped on Friday night. Since I disliked to make the hour-long drive to Owings Mill, Maryland alone, one of my sons would usually drive me over, hoping to pick up valuable advice about trends in the market on the way. Certain stocks jumped dramatically on Monday morning after being mentioned on that Friday night show.

We panelists were paid only $175 for expenses per telecast, and our firm names were not identified, but there were many fringe benefits. The group was very supportive, like an extended family, and we continued to help each other out through the years. Such well-known investors as Frank Capiello, Carter Randall, and Bob Nurock were early fellow panelists. The show provided us valuable name recognition. I was at the Beverly Wilshire Hotel swimming pool after one show, and so many people came up to me I felt like a movie star. (In March, 1992, I was the first woman inducted into the

"Wall $treet Week With Louis Rukeyser" Hall of Fame, along with such notables as Peter Lynch and Sir John Templeton.)

The Walshes' combined family had four young people graduating from high school in the 70s—Michael, Mark, Anne and Dan. (Mike wrote to his grandmother Curry after winning the achievement award in French at Georgetown Prep: "I've been working. You always thought I was too lazy to work, but I fooled you!")

I bought round-trip air tickets for the kids to backpack through Europe the summer of 1975 as their graduation presents. Their instructions were to call at American Express, General Delivery, to pick up small sums of money along the way when they ran short. (I thought that if I started out with too generous an amount to begin with, they might spend it all the first week.)

I met them in Munich, where we rented a Mercedes-Benz and with Mike as chauffeur, drove through Bavaria to Vienna. It was a different city from the one the Montgomery family visited after the war. For five days, we enjoyed the Opera House and other sights restored to their former grandeur. Then we joined a bus tour through the desolate and somewhat depressing Hungarian countryside. When we noticed a holiday celebration in one of the small villages on the outskirts of Budapest, the driver stopped so that we could watch the folk dancers. My young people could not resist hopping off the bus and joining in.

In Budapest, we attended Mass and took communion at the gilded altar of St. Stephen's Cathedral. It was a moving experience to watch the many hands reaching out to touch the ornate cross as the priest carried it down the central aisle. And there were other pleasures. We went back again and again to a famous coffee shop in the center city, where we devoured delicious calorie-filled pastries.

Having It All—A Woman In The New Era

Back in the U.S., I was pleased to see the country healing its wounds and leaving Watergate behind after President Richard M. Nixon's resignation, and Vice President Gerald

Julia Montgomery Walsh meets with President Jimmy Carter.

Ford's succession. I was elected to serve on the Board of Directors of the U.S. Chamber of Commerce in April 1976. When the Chamber asked me to head the special Judicial Review Committee to study privacy legislation, I achieved another "first," the first woman in the organization's history to serve as chairman of a standing committee.

The summer of 1976 marked a major milestone in our country's history. The Walshes were planning to celebrate the Bicentennial and the Fourth of July in New York, to view the stately procession of the Tall Ships from our balcony on the East River. Michael and I were driving to Manhattan in the blue Pontiac convertible, but we were running late. He made a wrong turn off the freeway, so we missed seeing the fireworks with the rest of the family.

That summer Michael became coordinator of supplies for the Democratic National Committee and had podium credentials for the Convention in Madison Square Garden. I had an opportunity to meet President-elect Jimmy Carter, and I was impressed by his warm handshake and friendly smile. As a member of the DNC Finance Committee, I made my contribution to the party, helping the Carter campaign to win the November election.

Later, as an elector for the District of Columbia in 1976, I was proud to cast a ballot for the Carter-Mondale ticket. A lifelong liberal Democrat, I envisioned that President Carter would support much-needed social programs in our country. At Christmas, the White House acknowledged my help during the campaign with a handsome greeting card signed by the President and First Lady Rosalyn Carter: "To Julia Walsh, with thanks and appreciation for your dedication and contributions to our country. We are proud to have served with you."

IV

My reward for serving was a three-year appointment to the board of the prestigious East-West Center at the University of Hawaii, to succeed Edgar F. Kaiser of Kaiser Industries. The Center was founded with the idea of exchanging technological and educational information between the U.S. and emerging Pacific Rim countries. (I had recognized early the changing focus in international business from Europe to the Far East.) The board was divided equally between Americans (both Democrats and Republicans) and foreign-born members, among them Japanese, Chinese, Pakistani and Indians, with one distinguished nuclear physicist from Australia.

My second visit to Honolulu gave me an opportunity to pay back a long overdue debt. I took my mother Kate Curry, who had never flown before, on the trip. We stayed at the Colony Surf Hotel where Tom and I had stopped over on our honeymoon, across from Kapiolani Park and next door to the "kamaina" establishment, the Outrigger Canoe Club. The breathtaking views of sunset over the Pacific from our oceanfront suite made Mother feel she really had come to the Paradise of the Pacific.

The Center held a reception and luau for the board members on the terrace of historic Washington House (now the Governor's Mansion), where Queen Emma was held prisoner during the U.S. Succession. Governor George Arioshi was there to place a lei of welcome around Mother's shoulders. She remembered meeting him on a recent visit to Millwood Lane, while attending a reception with me in Washington. Arioshi hooked his arm through Mother's and escorted her in to dinner. I think she was quite proud of the daughter who had made the trip possible.

Also during the Carter administration I was invited by General Calvin Franklin and the Air National Guard to join a group of community leaders (four women and eight men) on an inspection tour of the Panama Canal, soon to be turned over to the Panamanian government. Rioting spread through the streets while we were there, during which time we were forced to take refuge in the U.S. Embassy. I had never come so close to a mob before, and it was frightening to see what happens when a group of people lose control and participate in acts of violence they would never consider committing alone. Fortunately, our group was evacuated out the next day, and returned home unharmed.

Catholic Church activities always have been an important part of my life. With so many blessings to count, I've always felt I should pay back my dues. I was already serving on the board of the Shrine of the Immaculate Conception and as trustee of Georgetown University when William Cardinal Baum asked me to head the 1977–78 Cardinal's Appeal. I would be the first woman in the U.S. to head a major Catholic Diocesan appeal—quite a challenge. Our goal was to make over a million dollars for assorted Catholic charities, including many social services: youth education and pastoral counseling programs, day-care centers with medical attention for the elderly, a center for the deaf.

When the third Sunday in May rolled around, we had surpassed our goal, ringing in with a total of $1,025,926, the largest amount collected since the Appeal began. The next year we did it again. The famous trial lawyer, Edward Bennett Williams, kicked off the campaign in March with the theme of "Sharing God's Love." By May 1978, we had collected an even higher sum, $1,151,140!

Julia shows her devotion to the Catholic Church in many generous ways. In this photo she is seen with Cardinal William Baum and husband Tom.

Having It All—A Woman In The New Era

As a result of this labor of love, on Thanksgiving Thursday, 1978, I was awarded the President's Medal for Distinguished Community Service by the Catholic University of America. Among leaders of the Washington Community paid tribute to that evening was someone I very much admire, Father Gilbert Hartke. As founder of the Drama Department of Catholic University and the American College Theater Festival at Kennedy Center, and president of Ford's Theater, Father Hartke has made significant contributions to the cultural life of this city. I was very proud to be named along with him as one of those "citizens whose vision, hard work, and ability to solve problems has contributed to Washington's greatness."

In 1977, I was on President Carter's short list for the post of Secretary of Commerce, but lost out to Juanita Kreps, then president of Duke University, whose résumé included running a large corporation. Instead, the Administration offered me a seat on the Securities & Exchange Commission. In the end, I turned the position down, reluctantly. It required a five-year commitment, and a promise not to use the "revolving door" back into the securities industry for another four. The timing wasn't right. I was too young then to retire, and when I finished at age 59, I would be too old to develop another career. Yet I was ready to undertake a new challenge.

Starting something new in mid–life: Julia Walsh & Sons.

CHAPTER SEVEN

Julia Walsh & Sons

UNTIL I WAS 50-SOMETHING, I never thought
of starting my own business. Then I began to ask: why have I
stayed 22 years with the same firm? Most of the best analysts—
all men—had left. I could stay on forever as a loyal member of
a family-owned firm, but there was no room at the top. Then,
too, our business was changing. Instead of exclusively taking
orders for stocks and bonds, there were other investment
opportunities, such as real estate and oil and gas partnerships.
There were also important tax considerations. In the late 1970s,
the whole world was changing: the relationship of the securities industry to the economy, the relationship of the U.S. to the
rest of the world, plus the relationship of *women* to the world.

In spite of the strong "family" ties to the firm, I was growing
restless. Working as hard as I was, why should I be a high
profit center for someone else, instead of creating profits for
myself and my own children? I wanted to try something on my
own, to be my own boss. Because Ferris & Company was a
family business, and there were heirs, there was no opportunity
to build for my own family's future. The Ferrises would hate

to lose me, but I was sure they would understand my position. Thirty-five years before, George Ferris, Sr., the grand old man of the firm whom I greatly admire, followed the same line of reasoning when he started his own business.

One night in January 1977, my husband picked me up after work for a family dinner in Georgetown. My stepson Tom Walsh, my sons Michael and John, and "Alex" Armstrong, my assistant at Ferris, were with us. As we sat around the table brainstorming ideas, the older boys decided they were of an age to want to try our own business. John had joined me at Ferris, working as an analyst in the research department after completing the MBA program at NYU, and Tom D., after completing an MBA at Harvard Business School and with five years of experience with securities, was then corporate secretary of the National Association of Securities Dealers. We began to plan our new firm, Julia Walsh and *Sons*. After 20 years in the business, I wanted to prove that any woman with hard work and proper motivation could make a name for herself in a big way, as any man could. If I were ever going to take that "last chance leap," this was the time to do it.

I had a lot to risk, leaving a safe and profitable job to start something new in mid-life. In 1977, we had tuition to pay for four young people in college. But if you don't take risks, nothing big is going to happen. Nothing big may happen anyway, but if you don't try, you don't have a chance. Lucky for me, I did not have to start at Square One. I had established a customer-base in the Washington community and earned its respect and confidence, so my clients knew I was here to stay. A second factor gave me something solid to build on: I had accumulated enough capital to get through lean times. Third, and most important, I had winning products to sell. If I could see a certain stock was a winner, or a fantastic real estate deal was coming up, I shared this knowledge with my customers. I never recommended an investment that I myself had not put money in.

I was ready to take the plunge, to become one of the new breed of professional financial planning consultants. It was a proud moment in June 1977, when the name of the new company, JULIA WALSH & SONS, was placed in solid gold letters over the door of a suite of offices in the Barr Building facing Farragut Square (910 17th Street, NW) in downtown Washington. We held a huge meeting at the International Club to acquaint clients, old and new, with our firm. Louis Rukeyser was our guest speaker, offering his continuing support and encouragement.

My stepson, Thomas D. Walsh, was the obvious choice for president, and my son John Montgomery, former director of research at Ferris, was in line for vice president, director of research and portfolio manager. C. Alexandra Armstrong, who had spent 15 years learning the ropes at Ferris & Company, one of only 600 certified financial planners in the U.S. (the first *woman* CFP), was ready to assume full partnership.

My son Michael, then only 22, had been at Ferris as part-time research assistant since he was 14-years-old. (In those early years, I remember, when I gave him an investment account to study he immediately pointed out *my* mistake—I had forgotten to add the dividends!) He was then finishing a BA degree in accounting at the University of Virginia and planning to enter Georgetown Law School. He would be free to locate office space and do the necessary paper work with the Self Regulatory Organizations (SROs), such as the New York and American Stock Exchanges and the NASD.

"What do you call the head of your firm when she happens to be your mother?" asked my youngest son, Mark, who later joined up as a junior partner. "Mom" was ruled out, but Julia or Mrs. Walsh would do; most settled for Julia. The support team was very important. In my view, our people were much more

Julia Walsh & Sons

motivated because everyone in the new firm—including the clerical staff—participated in the profits. Everyone was *registered* at Julia Walsh & Sons. If a member of the firm wanted to invest his or her commission on a new stock, he or she was able to do so.

Soon after we started up, Henry T. ("Tom") Donaldson, a former associate at Ferris, came aboard as vice chairman, specializing in energy investments. For many of our clients, participation in oil and gas programs was an integral part of the investment strategy. Soon Robert J. Redpath came over from Whiteweld to join us as vice-president. Bob was a specialist in area markets, helping to identify the good investment potentials Washington has to offer. Metropolitan Washington continues to exceed the national average in the economic growth rate, has the highest average income, highest level of stock ownership, and the best education system of any major metropolitan area. This area in particular provided many unique and exciting real estate opportunities along with enticing venture capital investments.

Early on, Julia Walsh & Sons established exchanges with MBA programs at top universities throughout the country for summer interns, and from the beginning, we actively tried to hire and promote minorities.

Until I started my own firm, I had concentrated on account management. Now I had to start managing the business. I discovered the hard way that women heading their own companies are on call to make most of the day-to-day decisions. Will we need additional office space? How do we invest our cash? What safeguards can we build in to protect the business? I was fortunate from the beginning in being able to establish an arrangement to clear orders through Dean Witter & Company, thus eliminating the expense of back-office overhead and lowering labor costs.

We made no attempt at "glamour." My staff had my old settee and wing chair re-upholstered to match my deep-blue leather desk chair. I placed a watercolor of the White House signed by President Carter on the wall behind my desk, and on the opposite side, two etchings of Wall Street as it appeared in 1834 and 1856. We were ready to do business.

My first step was to outline a five-year plan. I saw our firm as a first-class medium-sized regional house to serve the needs of the Washington community. Our philosophy was that this is our town, we should work for it, work in it, contribute to it. In addition to the small individual investors I brought with me—the doctors, lawyers and business people investing their own money—we began to attract more small institutions and charities, such as St. Ann's Infant and Maternity Home, and organizations like the National Association of Women Business Owners (NAWBO).

I worked increasingly with the new breed of "Yuppies," two-career couples earning *amazing* salaries at a very early age. They wanted to know what to do with their money and how to protect it from the tax man. We began to investigate oil and gas and commercial real estate as tax shelters.

Our firm saw the most rapid expansion of any brokerage in the Washington area. We were fourth largest in revenues among the 22 Washington-based dealers in 1977. We saw our commissions grow from zero to $1.6 million a year. Portfolio management was our strength, and the firm produced rewarding results. In 1977 we managed $100 million in individual and small institutional funds. (In three representative portfolios for institutions, our returns on investment were 174 percent during the next three years, beating the Standard & Poor's 500 Index by a wide margin.)

In 1977, inflation was a monumental problem, and one reason for our success was that we advised clients to keep out of bonds, to invest in high-tech growth stocks that were the beneficiaries of inflation. We were willing to go out on a limb for oil stocks, gold and overseas investments. Our WRAP program (investment management for a flat annual fee), an idea inspired by John Montgomery, was a trend-setter and became a $100 billion business for the securities industry by the mid-90s.

It helped to concentrate on clients with similar goals, geared to capital gains and a certain risk level. With some 100 accounts doing relatively the same thing, it was easier to make day-by-day decisions. Networking was crucial. Many new clients —attorneys, accountants, and institutional investors— came from old clients who sent their friends to me. One of my biggest problems from the beginning was finding time for clients, the business, and my family without spreading myself too thin.

In the fall of 1978, my son Stephen was at the Dean Witter Training Center in San Francisco, staying with my old friend Mac MacCormac, who retired to the Bay Area. I stopped off after a business meeting and planned a nostalgic drive up the coast to Seattle with the two of them. My time, as always, was too short and the distance greater than I remembered. We never got to Seattle, but we had a great time together in the land of the giant redwoods before heading back to the city.

In November 1979, I went to Wall Street for the traditional welcome of our two-year-old firm on the Big Board. From its very beginning in 1792, the New York Stock Exchange had been an exclusively male domain, so I was very proud when JULIA WALSH & SONS flashed on the ticker tape around 10 A.M. At noon, the American Stock Exchange, of which we were associate members, gave a luncheon in my honor. Then I flew back to Washington to prepare for the annual convention of the Securities Industry Association the next day in Boca Raton, Florida.

Also in late 1979, *The Washingtonian* magazine sponsored an essay contest with the theme, "What is your favorite restaurant?" I couldn't resist putting in a good word for *my* favorite, Lion d'Or. Imagine my surprise when the editor rang up to say I won the prize: four-nights lodging at the Hotel George V in Paris, plus a gourmet dinner at a four-star restaurant, Chateau d'Artignan! Stephen and his fiancee, Beth Koehler, were planning their wedding for New Year's Eve, and what better way to start married life than a honeymoon in Paris? The prize was my wedding gift to them.

The economy took a downward turn in 1979, only two years after I started my business. The company had a lot at stake in energy and real estate investments when the market dropped dramatically. With all my assets on the block, for the second time in my life I was afraid I might fail. My health suffered again. A minor stroke at age 54 served as a warning that I'm not Superwoman.

But the market—and my good health—miraculously snapped back, and I began to feel like taking risks again. Broadening the business beyond stocks and bonds with a more profitable mix of managed accounts, we increased our revenue 500 percent. I re-learned two valuable lessons from the experience: the market is always subject to ups and downs, and it's smart to get away for a few days to relax whenever possible. The business and the household won't fall apart without me.

❧ II

If anybody had told me that by 1980 this country would not have passed the Equal Rights Amendment, I would have said it's not possible. In April of that year, when I was invited to give the keynote address at a convention of the American Association of University Women in Contra Mesa, California, "fairness" and "justice" were the key words for the weekend. We collected a great number of checks and cash to contribute toward ERA. The great majority of people in the U.S., men *and* women—over 70 percent—were for it; three-fourths of the population of this country in 35 states had ratified it. Both houses of Congress, the Senate and the House of Representatives overwhelmingly passed the ERA, but there was a powerfully financed opposition, and the Amendment went down in defeat despite our best efforts.

I told the 1,200 college graduates who attended the AAUW convention, most of them professionals, that it is time we women started handling our own business affairs. There is no way we are ever going to accomplish anything unless we gain economic and political clout. We have been taught to play it safe, not to take risks. But with economic independence comes freedom and power. I hope my talk was sufficiently inspiring to young women following in my career path.

Among the burgeoning network of organizations for business women springing up in this era was the Women's Economic Round Table, founded in 1978 by Maria Rolfe in memory of her husband, economist Sidney Rolfe. I have been an active member of this group since its founding. Its objective is to educate the public about economics, business and finance. (One recent topic under discussion was political advertising for the 1996 presidential campaign, with panelists Robert H. Ryan, campaign manager for Governor Pataki of New York in '94, Rob Sephardson, a leading advertising spokesman concerned with corporate and issues advocacy, and Jerry Della Femina, outspoken critic of political advertising.)

The world changed a lot in the decade of the 80s. In my view, it is very important for women to prepare for future changes. We are no longer the exception but the rule in business. One of the most satisfying experiences of my life was to help to establish a graduate program in management for women at Simmons College in Boston. Higher earnings are the unequivocal measure of success, and for 26- to 32-year-olds who want to build solid careers in the field of business, the master's degree is a necessity. Some ten years after the program was established, Simmons MBA's were entering the job market on the same pay scale as the men and women from Stanford and Harvard.

Back in Washington, groundbreaking for the new Convention Center took place in April 1980. By this time, the J.W. Marriott Hotel and the newly-renovated National Press Building complex with the shops at National Place were beginning to make downtown D.C. a "people place" again. We were hoping the new Center would expand the city's revenue base and provide more jobs, with a resurgence of new luxury hotels, rentals, and other development in the area.

In the summer of 1980, after a business trip to inspect Pitney Bowes facilities on the Continent, I flew to Ireland with Tom and young Peggy to see the home of my ancestors for the first time. We could see why it is called the "Emerald Isle," with vast greenery as far as the eye can see. We spent only a few days in Dublin, but planned to return for a longer visit with the family.

In 1981, among other activities, I went to Minneapolis/St. Paul to speak on "Business and Productivity" at the Fifth Anniversary celebration of the Twin Cities Conference. In the same year, I also served as Director of District 10 of the National Association of Securities Dealers, of which our firm is a member. At a banquet sponsored by the sales and marketing executives of Washington, I was named Metropolitan Washington Sales Executive of the Year (the same evening that Lt. General James H. Doolittle was honored with the Distinguished Service Award, and radio station WMAL's Frank Harden was presented an Award for Community Service.)

The year 1982 was another full and busy one. In January, I was invited to attend the "Banquet of the Golden Plate" at the Breakers Hotel in Palm Beach, as one of the business leaders to be honored by the Northwood Institute. Arthur Rubloff, international realtor and developer, and Thomas A. Carvel, the ice-cream industry tycoon, were among the honorees, and only two women, Muriel Kauffman of Marion Laboratories in Kansas, and myself. (Former Senator Margaret Chase Smith won the award the year before.)

I received requests to speak to many groups and business organizations. In February, my son John and I were in Boca Raton, Florida, where I addressed the annual meeting of the Commodities Futures Trading Association (CFTA). I was also honored to be keynote speaker at the Executive Round Table of the Graduate School of Management, College of Special Programs, at my alma mater, Kent State. My topic was "The Investment Climate: A Washington Point of View." I am always happy to boost my adopted city.

The "Topping Out" ceremony for the new Washington Convention Center was held on May 26, 1982. In December, I was honored guest at the George Washington University Club luncheon for "Women of Achievement," to reward my efforts as the new Center's director. The Ribbon-Cutting and reception on December 10 was a proud time for the District, with Mayor Marion Barry, Jr. and board chairman Edward A. Singletary on hand to welcome the VIPs, and the Honorable Walter E. Fauntroy, D.C. delegate to the House of Representatives, offering the prayer of dedication. Twenty-five new construction contracts were already underway, totaling approximately $55 million in revenue. (Ten of these contracts, totaling $25 million, were placed with minority-owned firms or joint ventures, and minorities constituted 61 percent of the payroll.) It was expected that the Center would attract some 300,000 convention delegates annually. Revenues from the out-of-town visitors would bring new dollars into Washington and expand the local economy and tax base.

One morning I was surprised when I picked up the *Washington Post* Sunday magazine section with my face on the cover, along with local business leaders J.W. "Bill" Marriott, head of the giant hotel and catering chain, Harold Hall, president of Southern Railroad, and Riggs Bank president Joe Allbritton (our former neighbor at Walmont). I was the only woman.

My life was not all work and no play. As a result of a sales contest sponsored by National Resource Management, an oil production company, with a little bit of luck I won a Bermuda vacation at the beautiful Coral Beach Club. This time, it was John's and Stephen's turn to enjoy a holiday with me.

During this era, I was so blessed by good luck I wanted to share it. My loyal sales assistant, Jane Wyman, and I flew to New York to attend a dinner meeting of the Women's Equity Action League, at which I would receive the "Big Weal" award. After the meeting, it was time to reward Jane's "ten years of loyal service." I presented her with two round-trip airline tickets to Hawaii, where she and her husband were treated to a royal tour of Honolulu by Bob Hewett, special assistant to the president and corporate secretary of the East-West Center.

When I became a member of the board of the National Symphony Orchestra, our family had the use of a choice box for concerts at Kennedy Center. Sally Chapotin was chairperson of the Symphony Ball that year, which I attended with Tom in white-tie. The theme was Italian, with Ambassador Rinaldo Petrignani and his wife on hand to welcome guests to a delicious "pranza." Antipasto, capellini, and arriosto de vitello were served in a Italian piazza setting among papiermaché horses, fountains, and Roman columns. What a surprise when the Walshes won the door prize, a gray Fiat Strata! We turned it over to Peggy, Jr., the youngest member of the family, who had reached the age when wheels of her own were a necessity.

My kids were impressed when I met my first big-name movie star at a USO luncheon at Ft. McNair. Senator John Warner and his beautiful wife, Elizabeth Taylor, were there to "Save the Bald Eagle," on the verge of extinction. Her violet eyes looked tired and Liz, a bit bored, as well she might have been, after so many political rallies that season. Sometime later, I met the former Grace Kelly, then Princess Grace of Monaco, in Washington for an official State visit, at a State Department reception. Her tragic death on the Grand Corniche occurred soon after.

When Tom Walsh and I were invited to the launching of the "Lady Baltimore" cruise ship, we joined other local VIPs on a special train back to Washington, with a five-piece band on board to serenade us enroute. When we arrived at the welcoming reception in the Executive Office Building I remembered that—more than 40 years before—I held my first full-time job there at the State Department! A dinner dance on the roof garden of the Washington Hotel, with its unrivaled view of the White House and Mall, ended another memorable evening.

During the Christmas season, Julia Walsh & Sons sponsored the production of "The Snow Goose" on WETA, our local public television station. We used the holiday program as the cover of our company Christmas card.

When I was invited to the founding meeting of the "Committee of 200" in Los Angeles, the Business Roundtable—the most prominent group for corporate executives at that time— excluded women members. Some 21 of the top female executives throughout the country decided that women should have a similar business forum of their own. The organizers spent nine months tracking down the names of hundreds of women bosses, mostly from the membership lists of the National Association of Women Business Owners.

To qualify for that organization, a women must be in charge, wholly or in part, of a company whose sales are at least $5 million annually, or manage operations with budgets of that size in larger firms. Strong individualists all, many of these busy women executives shied away from joining other groups. Some 40 percent turned down the first invitation. But the Committee of 200 that finally came together represented a stellar collection of female executive talent, from a wide mixture of industries and regions of the U.S. They ranged in age from their 20s to their 70s, came from 30 states and 70 kinds of businesses; from Katharine Graham, chairman of The Washington Post Company, to Christie Hefner, the 29-year-old corporate vice president and heir apparent of Playboy Enterprises. Despite initial doubts, the organizational meeting was a great success, and the women bosses almost universally praised the Committee as a source of networking and support. Some of the younger members acknowledged that they felt, for the first time, that it was O.K. to be successful. (Our efforts were noticed by Washington *Dossier* magazine, which sent a photographer to catch me with another member of the Committee, Adrienne Arsht Feldman.)

Through the years, the Committee of 200 Foundation has provided scholarship programs for women business students, educational programs to promote entrepreneurship coordinated with major universities, and lending programs to provide start-up capital for businesses owned by women. Another concern has been to provide women on state and federal subsidies with the education and skills to achieve financial independence. But the Committee has dedicated its major efforts to recognizing and fostering entrepreneurship among women in business.

✤III

When the American Association of University Women honored me with its Highest Achievement Award for "significant contributions" in the field of business, I was on a visit to the Far East with Dr. Victor Li, President of the University of Hawaii's East-West Center, and other members of that board. My acceptance speech was video-taped from Tokyo. I donated the $3,000 prize that went with the Award to set up a scholarship fund (at the university of their choice) for a young woman entering business.

Peggy Jr., her only daughter, on an East-West Center trip with Julia.

Peggy, Jr., who finished at Holton Arms School in June, went with me on the trip as a graduation present. Our first stop was Hong Kong, where we stayed in the old Peninsula Hotel with an unrivaled view of the harbor, and took time to shop for bargains at the world-famous shopping arcades of Kowloon. We enjoyed a Peking duck dinner in the home of a young partner in the Carruthers brothers' law firm of Washington, a former aide to Admiral Elmo Zumwalt, my associate in "Project Hope." Then Peggy and I traveled to Portuguese Macau, with the famous gambling casinos. The train ride through the rice paddies of southern China opened our eyes to a world we had never glimpsed before.

When we arrived in Canton, we toured the carefully preserved home of Sun-Yat-Sen, former Premier of China. We both agreed that this was one of the significant highlights of our trip. It was my first visit to the Orient, and my impression was of a heavily populated beehive. The crowds in the city streets on an average day far outnumbered holiday shoppers pushing and shoving their way down Fifth Avenue in New York. In some of the smaller cities of China, we had the uneasy experience of being stared at as the only Western women in the streets.

When we crossed the Straits of Malaysia, vast plantations of rubber stretched out before us, and I had the opportunity to survey the rubber industry for the first time. This was of great interest to someone who spent her early years within shouting distance of the Goodyear plant and whose first investment was Goodyear stock.

In every country we visited companies and witnessed first-hand the vast trading empire of the Japanese. In my view, there were many emerging market opportunities in the region, and I urged the Board to recognize that the future was—and is—looking toward the East.

The members of the board were greeted enthusiastically and invited to lunch by the Chamber of Commerce of Tokyo. The Japanese Chamber—all men—were surprised to discover that our group included a woman. In Japan, women still play only supporting roles in business. Dr. Li refused to attend the luncheon if I were not invited, so an exception was made—another "first" for Julia. We received cordial and genuine hospitality in Japanese homes we visited; our hosts couldn't have been more accommodating. They surfeited us with sushi and other

Julia Walsh & Sons

unusual raw fish dishes until most of us longed for a good old-fashioned hamburger. We visited Kyoto, another major business city, and I was happy to take time out to view the ancient shrines and learn about the Japanese culture.

Bangkok was one of my favorite cities, a thriving, progressive metropolis that retained its mix of ancient architecture and exotic customs. I loved watching the long boats plying their way through the klongs [canals]. Often the quickest way to get from one point to another in the crowded inner city was in the motorized rickshaws (called "tuk-tuks", after the clacking sound of their motors). The Oriental Hotel is rated one of the world's finest, and I soon discovered why. My travel-weary laundry was returned within 12 hours in individual plastic wraps, with a spray of baby orchids on top of the box!

Mac MacCormac, my friend from Munich days, then living in Bangkok, invited us to dinner one evening. We took a launch across the canal to a pagoda where we deposited shoes at the door and sat on cushions around a low table. During the traditional Thai dinner of many courses, ritual dancers performed their native dances in colorful costumes.

The next day, he took us to the Jim Thompson house, an enclave of thatch-roofed buildings on one of the canals. We had heard all about the Thompson case from my partner, Tom (Thompson) Donaldson. The mysterious disappearance of his uncle without a trace in the northern provinces of Thailand is still a matter of conjecture, though the general consensus is that he was murdered while on assignment with the CIA. His house is maintained as a museum of Thai culture, the table still set for dinner as it was the day he left. The Thais are an exceptionally warm and hospitable people; to say that we were treated like queens is a cliché, but true.

Peggy and I left Bangkok reluctantly on the last lap of our journey. Our relationship had progressed from one of teenage conflict with a parent to a mature friendship between two adults. We still laugh at some of the scenes during our trip: fighting about the scary driver of a rickety car in Bangkok who, Peggy was convinced, was going to kill us and leave us by the side of the road. She wasn't too enthusiastic about a four-hour bus ride across Fiji to surprise the governor of the islands for lunch. But when snorkeling off a deserted island in the South Pacific, my 18-year-old admitted there were fringe benefits of having a mother with a successful career. This trip cemented the mother-daughter bond forever.

When we returned, having observed first-hand how the average woman lives in the Far East, I appreciated more than ever the increased opportunities for women in my own country. While many Americans see only the problems in the U.S., those of us who travel extensively realize that our country is far ahead of everyone else's—in virtually all areas.

At this time, the U.S. Office of Education was inaugurating an international campaign to fight hunger and poverty in the Third World and to heighten awareness of the plight of women in underdeveloped countries. I agreed to co-chair an OEF International group to study these issues with Richard Lugar, chairman of the Senate Foreign Relations Committee. I was reminded again of the great gap between opportunities for women in those countries and in our own when I went to Cape Canaveral to watch the first American woman, Sally Ride, launched into orbit!

Some time later, David Linowes asked me to join the commission he was heading to study the fair market value of coal leases for President Ronald Reagan and the U.S. Department of the Interior. I agreed reluctantly to serve on that obscure body for a Republican administration, largely because of long-standing ties with Linowes and the Democratic Party. His brother Robert Linowes was a past president of the Washington Board of Trade, and another brother, Sol Linowitz, held many important posts in the diplomatic field. In spite of the fact that it was a very busy time in the market, as a loyal Democrat I considered I was doing my civic duty. When I was sworn in at the White House on

"A black, a woman, two Jews and a cripple."

August 24, 1983, I never dreamed I would be catapulted onto front-page news two weeks later. When Secretary James G. Watt announced his appointments, he made the highly-publicized statement that his Commission was composed of "every kind of a mixture you can have— a black, a woman, two Jews and a cripple. And we have talent." That foot-in-the-mouth remark was covered nationwide by the media and cost him his job. He was right about talent.

Groundbreakers all, the men and women on the Commission defied categorization: Andrew F. Brimmer (black), David F. Linowes (Jewish), Donald C. Alexander (a WASP, who joked, "The Secretary might have thought I'm *mentally* handicapped"), Richard Gordon (Jewish, his right arm paralyzed from polio), and myself (female). Watt called me the next day to apologize and said he preceded and followed that statement with nice things to say about all of us—true, if you saw the whole quote—but the media picked up only on that one line.

This was one of the most complex situations I ever got myself into. I spent the next three or four days facing reporters and television cameras. The Commission's first hearing on Capitol Hill had attracted some two dozen people. The hearing that came after the incident brought out nearly one hundred, including television crews with their blinding lights. (A full-page color spread in January 1984 *Life* magazine featured our smiling faces.) After that experience, I always introduced myself at lectures with the proud announcement: "I am *that woman!*"

Watt's remarks brought public attention to the Commission, but in my view, it would have been better left alone. It was an ironic precursor to the affirmative action and political correctness of today. The liberals had been (justifiably) after Watt for some time, and got him with this flip comment which, in retrospect, seems quite tame.

The Commission was a very obscure little body, composed of academics and economists, with no political bias. Our homework involved finding out what was being done about the coal-leasing issue, since the government owns more than 80 percent of the coal deposits in the U.S., primarily in Wyoming, Utah, Montana, and North and South Dakota. (As a nation, we own 60 percent of the coal deposits in the entire world.) Dramatic changes were taking place in the U.S.: technology was slowly but surely replacing heavy industry, and energy conservation reduced coal consumption by nearly one-third, so future planning was a major part of our job.

That was the summer of my honorary degrees. At their 105th Commencement, I finally received a degree—an honorary one!—from Smith College, the one I had hoped to attend as an undergraduate. At Colby College in New Hampshire I was honored also for my contributions in the world of business.

In June 1983, I also returned to Kent State University for the first time in many years for the Commencement exercises. My son John and his daughter, my namesake Julia, went with me. We stayed at the family home on Preston Avenue with "Grandma" Curry. I was especially happy that my mother could be with me to share this triumph, for she died only two years later. While John and I were at Kent State, we participated in setting up the KSU Foundation. Julia Walsh & Sons was heavily invested at the time in gold and other companies in South Africa. We faced an unforeseen controversy on campus, sparked by students and other liberal elements who protested a donation to the school of "tainted" money. We soon sold out our investments in gold, not because of the protest, but because these holdings ceased to be sound investments. The stocks had done extremely well, but more important, we sensed that the inflation outlook now favored financial assets as inflation hedges.

Julia and her mother, "Kate" Curry.

One of the great moments of my life came when President Michael Schwartz presented me with an Honorary Doctor of Laws degree from my alma mater. He said some very nice things about me at the presentation: "This remarkable woman possesses a rare combination of energy, dedication, and good humor. She is a dynamic and positive role model for today's young women." I particularly like being a "role model" for young women of today. We have made progress, but we still

Risks & Rewards

have a long way to go. In my view, women contribute a special sensitivity to business, because of where we come from, and because we see things differently in a male-oriented world. If I have accomplished anything worthwhile in my life, it is to have shown the next generation of women that with hard work and a little bit of luck they, too, can make it.

✤IV

In 1983, our firm reached another milestone. It was obvious that Julia Walsh & Sons could no longer operate as we had in the past. To do a good job, we had to offer an increasingly wider array of products to remain a full-service firm, or become a "boutique." We had foreseen the future demise of limited partnerships, and felt that smaller capital stocks were peaking. The buy-outs and mergers of such companies as Prudential-Bache, Dean Witter/Sears, and Drexel-Burnham during 1982-83 convinced me that we could sell out at that time to an advantage with a greater multiple of book value. As Lasky (and John Montgomery) pointed out, when the customers are at the door with blank checks in hand, it's time to sell.

After extensive research, we decided to merge with a 90-year-old Boston brokerage, Tucker Anthony & R.L. Day, a subsidiary of the John Hancock Mutual Life Insurance Company. We had many close ties with that firm; two friends from John Hancock drove Michael to the University of Virginia for Commencement. (Michael was the first of the "Sons" to leave the family firm; in 1980, he joined the New York Stock Exchange, then later moved on to Goldman-Sachs.)

The papers were signed. I would continue to be Managing Director of the new firm, operating under the original name, bringing with me some 4,000 clients. For his part, Ward Carey, CEO of Tucker Anthony, was acquiring a compatible client base and entering the highly-profitable Washington market. I felt that I had the best of all worlds when we moved into a handsome building at 1050 Connecticut Avenue, one of Washington's most prestigious addresses, with Duke Ziebert's restaurant on the ground floor. At that time, our firm was managing more than $200 million in assets.

Just when I resolved to take life easier, my name was proposed as president-elect of the Greater Washington Board of Trade. My husband Tom Walsh held that office in 1963, when I served as his "first lady." (One of the highlights of Tom's presidency was a luncheon for Charles A. Lindbergh at the Mayflower Hotel, when his wife, Anne Morrow Lindbergh, received an award from Georgetown University.) I had been active in that organization since 1965, but in its 96-year history, the presidency had never been offered to a woman. I understood what a challenge I was undertaking, but thought I could make a real contribution.

When the Board of Trade was formed in 1889, Washington lacked water filtration and an adequate sewer system, and railroad tracks on the Mall marred the city's landscape. Flooding transformed unpaved streets into muddy bogs, and malaria was prevalent. With no public library, municipal building, hospital, or safe bridge across the Potomac River, the capital city wasn't a pleasant place in which to live or to do business. Washingtonians had no federal representation until the Board—after years of effort beginning in 1910—formalized the Joint Citizen's Committee for National Representation and succeeded in ratifying the 23rd Amendment (1961) which permitted District citizens to vote for the first time in Presidential elections. When I first came to Washington, it was a much smaller, sleepy, southern city in which the primary industry was government. It almost closed down in summertime when Congress went into recess. (That was also before the Kennedy Center brought world-class performers to the capital.) When I became president of the Board of Trade in 1985, it was my goal to make Washington a world leader in business, industry, and banking.

The 96th annual meeting was held at the new J.W. Marriott Hotel. I had studied the city from several angles and decided that its problems couldn't be solved by government alone. First on my agenda was to expand the private sector. Washington was not a venture capital city, like Silicon Valley. I knew that it would be useful to form a closer alliance with the Washington/Baltimore Regional Association to compete with other metropolitan areas in attracting new businesses. In the first year, we allocated an additional $100,000 in funds for that purpose.

We began by sending additional domestic trade missions throughout the U.S. in an effort to encourage West Coast and Mid-Western businesses to relocate in the Washington area. For their orientation, we initiated the "Executour" program, a two-day invitational bus tour of industrial sites in the District for busy executives. (The Mid-Atlantic president of MCI, Brian Thompson, later commented: "We planted our seed in Washington, and it grew!")

Continuing with an earlier program to attract new businesses from abroad, I went with the Board on a 1983 mission to Europe. We specifically wanted to lure high-technology firms to Washington. We visited Switzerland and Germany and got some nibbles from companies that wanted to take a look at the area.

Transportation had always been a major priority of the Board. In the early days, the Board helped to expand the street railway system and lobbied for the construction of Union Station. Bridges across the Potomac were hazardous and in poor repair until the Board promoted the Arlington Memorial Bridge and others. In 1928, the Board was the first organization to call for a local airport at Gravelly Point—now National Airport—and later to secure approval for Dulles International. In my time, the Board formed a permanent transportation committee to act as convener/facilitator to coordinate with other groups; Ed Colodny, then chairman of USAir, was chosen to head the committee. (One goal was a takeover of the regional airports; we negotiated with then-Secretary of Transportation Elizabeth Hanford Dole to get Uncle Sam out of the local airport business.) In 1967, the Board started studying the feasibility of a subway system which preceded the construction of Metrorail, so essential for the area's economic growth.

We also tried to broaden the approach to unemployment by analyzing the larger unemployment picture in the Greater Washington area, to see how the business community could become more involved. Until that time, the Board worked with summer programs only, such as the "Summer Jobs for Youth" campaign. I helped to bring on-line training into the public schools to help students prepare for better permanent jobs. We also studied safety issues in the workplace and workmen's compensation.

The District Zoning Commission had been created in 1922, to help formulate regulations for future building. Zoning became a crucial issue during my era on the Board, with so much new construction in the central city. There was only so much land, and a fight was waged between the builders and developers on the one hand, and those of us who thought it necessary to limit growth.

The Board also was responsible for the codification of District laws in my era. We established the "one day, one trial" rule for the jury system. In addition, the Public Safety Committee initiated an anti-crime campaign, with a well-organized Neighborhood Watch program. At Christmas time when shoplifting, bad checks and credit card abuse were rampant, the Board added to holiday security details in the

Faye Bates, Governor Celeste, and Julia at Ohio Women's Hall of Fame presentation.

city's retail stores. We also initiated a program of awarding Gold Medals of Valor to fire-fighters and police officers who risked their lives in making Washington a safer city. (Some years before, Tom Walsh had helped to organize HEROs, Inc.; the Gold Medals were the logical next step.) I was pleased with the progress the Board was making with minorities. The president-elect to succeed me in 1986 was Roger Blunt, an African-American, president of the Tyroc Construction Company. Having been the "token" woman on several business task forces and boards, I was happy to see that 50 percent of the Board of Trade members working with me were women.

January 1985 heralded the 50th Inaugural of an American President. Republicans—Ronald Reagan and his wife Nancy—would again be the occupants of the White House. The Board was responsible for planning the parade and festivities that involved some 300,000 people and a financial outlay of some $30 million. Among other vital statistics, there were 4,000 police officers assigned to the streets, some 200,000 soft drinks supplied and 30 tons of ice! (Remembering the snow-bound streets when my son John marched in the John F. Kennedy Inaugural parade, I also took the precaution of recommending seven miles of snow fence along the parade route.) Though no snow fell, it was so cold on Inaugural Day that the festivities were moved to the Capital Center in Landover, Maryland.

Julia Walsh & Sons

Later that year I received two more honorary degrees: the first from Marymount College of Virginia, the second from Marietta College in Ohio. On Founders' Day, President Sherrill Cleveland of Marietta presented me with my 12th honorary degree. (His wife was Betty Chorpenning who attended Akron's East High School in the Class of 1943.) I credit the good preparation I received there and at the Kent State Business School for much of my success. I was especially proud to be inducted into the Women's Hall of Fame in my native state of Ohio, with then-Governor Celeste making the presentation.

Another honor came in 1985 when I was designated a Dame of the Sovereign Military Hospitaller Order of St. John of Jerusalem, Rhodes and Malta, commonly known as the "Knights of Malta." This Catholic organization provides support for a wide variety of charities in the Washington area: Providence Hospital, Georgetown Cancer Home Care, a home visitors' program, a residence for older women, and SHARE, an organization that provides supplemental food for needy families. It also takes part in many international programs.

The largest spiritual activity of the Order is the annual pilgrimage to the Shrine at Lourdes, which Tom and I joined in 1990. Bishop Baum of the Washington diocese, moving to the Vatican after becoming Cardinal that year, traveled with us. We were invited to attend a private audience of only 100 with Pope John Paul II in the garden of the Castel Gandolfo. To kiss the hand of one of the great spiritual leaders of our century was a profoundly moving privilege for me.

In Rome, we stayed at the Hotel Hassler at the top of the Spanish Stairs. My old friend from the Foreign Service, Carmen Bucher Wirth, co-owner of the Hassler, heard that it was Tom's birthday. She brought out vintage champagne for the celebration on the Hassler roof garden that evening, with the magnificent panorama of the Eternal City spread out before our eyes. I always find it hard to believe I am actually there, in such a dreamlike setting.

In June 1987, Kay Landen, president of the National Association of Bank Women, invited me to attend the third anniversary awards dinner at the Grand Hyatt Hotel in New York City. This salute to senior financial women, all leaders and innovators in the financial services industry, would benefit the NABW Foundation.

An exciting end to an exciting decade was an invitation from then-Secretary of Defense Casper Weinberger to join the 51st Joint Civilian Orientation Conference on an inspection tour of military installations around the U.S. We traveled from Camp Hood, Texas, where we checked out the FF100 fighter planes, to San Diego, California, where we went aboard an aircraft carrier. The trip was a bit strenuous for my aging bones, but I pulled on khaki trousers and did my best to keep up with "the boys." They presented me with a photo album with my name inscribed in gold letters as a remembrance of the trip.

Julia Walsh: a role model for future generations.

CHAPTER EIGHT

My Life's Greatest Challenge

AFTER JULIA WALSH & SONS merged with Tucker Anthony, and my term as president of the Board of Trade was behind me, I felt free to focus on the investment business again and to become an "elder" of the women's movement.

In March 1991, I became involved in another activity that gave me deep satisfaction and further opportunities to travel to Eastern Europe. Republican President George Bush appointed me—a lifelong Democrat and the only woman—to serve on the board of the Czecho-Slovak American Enterprise Fund. Because the work of returning the formerly Communist countries to privately-owned business and industry was such a multi-layered process, top executives from a cross-section of fields were appointed to the Fund: Committee chairman John R. Petty, former CEO of Marine Midland Bank; David Maxwell, former chairman of Fannie Mae; Charles Vanig, who spent two dozen years as an Ohio Congressman and then joined Squire, Sanders & Dempsey, as an attorney; and Milan Andrus, a retired industrialist, VP of the FMC corporation. We five American members of the Fund would be joined by

Czech and Slovak representatives at a later date. The initial grant to support this private sector development was a mere $5 million in the beginning, appropriated from the Foreign Affairs Operations Bill. The Administration would be asking a total of $60 million later from Congress.

During his visit to Prague that year, President Bush delivered the message that the Fund was designed "to help unleash the creativity and drive of the Czech and Slovak peoples" to build a free market economy and stable economic rule. On each of three trips to the former Iron Curtain countries—Hungary, Poland, and Czechoslovakia—the other board members and I visited factories and industrial shows to see how these satellite countries were faring after the departure of the Soviets.

On one of our visits, the delegation met with the President of the Czech Republic, Vaclav Havel. I was much impressed by this intellectual professor, diplomat and political leader who had such a sound grasp of the realities of business. President Havel also recognized that there were pressing environmental concerns, given the extent of pollution in these countries that still relied on heavy industry. While working to provide clean air and clean water, the Fund could also create opportunities for investment. It was an exciting time to be there, and we could see that we had a rare opportunity to make a difference.

The Czecho-Slovak question has always been part of the larger, more complicated problem of Central, Eastern, and Southeastern Europe. Its roots lie in the historic background of these two ethnic groups: the Slovaks, a slavic people to the East of the Czechs, were early united with them in the kingdom of Greater Moravia, but later were separated under the conquering Magyars of Hungary. Differences developed between the Czechs, outside of the Kingdom, and the Slovaks, within Hungary. The Slovaks, who had no opportunity to develop their own culture and written language and who had no political institutions of their own, moved into the mountain areas and became peasants and hill folk, dependent on the the prosperous Magyars and bankers in Budapest.

Prague was becoming the capital of Western Slavdom as early as 1910, when Slovak leaders first moved into the towns and were beginning to attend the University of Prague, where Czech was the required language. Germans also moved into Slovak territory, bringing Lutheran Protestantism, whereas the Czechs kept to their Roman Catholicism.

The years 1914–1918 saw the struggle for Czechoslovak independence under the inspired Czech leader, Thomas G. Masaryk. Masaryk was convinced that, if joined by the Slovaks, Czechoslovakia could become a strong and independent country. The Treaty of Versailles at the end of World War I united the two peoples, and Czechoslovakia enjoyed the longest period of between-the-wars multi-party democracy in Central Europe. Then German troops marched into Prague in March 1939 to establish a Czech "Protectorate," dividing it again from the Republic of Slovakia. General George Patton liberated— and reunited—the two countries in 1945. Sadly, Czechoslovakia fell into the clutches of the Russian bear at Yalta. Then just as the Czechs were beginning to achieve limited independence within the Soviet Union, the Red Army moved into Prague in the tragic spring of 1968.

After the separation of the Czech and Slovak Republics again in 1992, in my view, the Czech Republic is still the most progressive and hopeful of the former Iron Curtain countries. The citizens have retained their self-respect, and are well-known for being hard-working and industrious. From 1948 to 1988, there was no private industry, but after the Communists withdrew, the Czechs rushed to return to a market economy.

Czechoslovakia was never bombed during the war, so it had an efficient distribution system and a relatively solid base for reviving capitalism. But the Communist government left virtually no infrastructure with which to make the transition.

My Life's Greatest Challenge

The country needed up-to-date professional expertise and a financial leg up. The Fund was established to help arrange joint ventures, to create loan packages, make equity investments, and assist in privatization.

There are two on-site offices, one in Prague and one in Bratislava, staffed by U.S. research teams who sift through thousands of proposals. The staff selects 20 or 30 projects each year, including "big business" (by Czech standards), such as convenience foods, musical instruments and conversion of former munitions factories to commercial heavy industry. Among smaller industries are such projects as hydroelectric power plants and a new and burgeoning ski resort business, plus numerous Mom-and-Pop enterprises. For instance, the number of bakeries is increasing rapidly—and many of the bakers are women!

In the summer of 1991, Tom Walsh and I had an opportunity to make one of our early dreams come true. Since the time of our marriage, we threatened to rent a castle and take the kids back to Ireland, the land of our ancestors. It became a running joke in the family. When one of our son Tom's business connections, an Irish industrialist and CEO of Darby's Irish Cream, offered to rent us a large Tudor house in a suburb of Dublin, we jumped at the chance. We invited all of the children, their spouses, and the grandchildren to stay with us some time during the two summer months. Eleven out of 12 visited us, many with their families. Peggy left her temporary job to spend more time with her parents in Ireland. Rob Cornog, her fiancé, was calling every night while she was there, so it became obvious that we would soon have another son-in-law in the family.

We had to stagger schedules in order to accommodate different vacation times and interests. My brother Ed Curry and his wife Betty flew in from California. Tom's son Dan and his wife Helene were already there. Stephen, Mark and Anne arrived on the same flight, accompanied by Mac MacCormac. Mac brought with him two old friends from Munich, the Princesses Eleanora and Dorothea von Bayern. We were happy to reciprocate the royal hospitality offered to us in Munich during the 1972 Olympics. While Mac was with us, we celebrated his 85th birthday with a Zacher Torte imported from Vienna for that very special occasion. There was something for everyone—a swimming pool (possibly the coldest in the universe), very fine courses nearby for the golfers, and for the grand-children, donkey carts. We explored the historic sites in Dublin, such as King's College, and took in a performance at the world-famous Abbey Theater. A highlight was the Fourth of July celebration at the Embassy, where we joined other Americans for the big party of the year.

Tom and I drove to the Dingle Peninsula on the West Coast to look up his cousin, Dan Walsh, in County Kerry. Dan's business was tractors, and a thriving one it was, with all the good rich farm-land nearby. He and his family lived in an old stone house facing the ocean, where we were warmly welcomed. There was a fairly steady to-and-fro between County Kerry and Dublin during that two-month period. (Dan and his wife later visited us in Washington.)

Back home on September 15, I attended the opening school Mass at Seton Hall College with my cousin Jim Mooney's wife, a Seton Hall alumna. The Seton Medal is awarded to women whose achievements parallel the life of St. Elizabeth. I never considered my life "saintly," but I have always tried to live by the Golden Rule. I was proud to be listed along with honorees Rose Kennedy, Mrs. Bob Hope, and noted Catholic authors, educators and leaders of charitable organizations.

I hoped to give a lesson on lifemanship to the girls when I told them that the worst mistake a woman can make is to turn her money over to someone else to manage. On that day, however, I tried not to lecture them too much about money—in the presence of Mother Seton! I see some alarming trends in American society today, so my principal message was about family values and ethical concerns in business and government.

In 1990, I was invited to a fund-raiser at the home of Pamela Harriman in Georgetown to fill the Democratic war chest. I hoped that we could make a difference in the next election. We did! In January 1993, William Jefferson "Bill" Clinton was inaugurated President of the United States, and for the first time in many years a Democrat would be occupying the White House. My son Mark and I were guests at the victory dinner for the new President. We were also present when President Clinton stopped at the first Inaugural Ball to be held in the new Convention Center.

In March 1992, Felice Schwartz, president and founder of Catalyst, asked me to join past and present award winners on the dais at the Annual Awards Dinner at the Waldorf-Astoria Hotel. I was happy to be present on this festive occasion to mark women's progress in business. For more than three decades, Catalyst has conducted pioneering research and provided guidance to corporations on the career development of women. Its mission has been to provide women with options, so they can do what they choose with their lives.

That was a good time to reflect on the major changes in women's lives that have taken place since 1962. Women have advanced in large numbers from the lower levels of the corporate and professional communities into positions of power and leadership. In recent years, Catalyst has taken steps to remove the more subtle barriers to women's achievement. It launched the first national study of part-time work, job-sharing, and tele-commuting arrangements at the managerial and professional levels to determine the impact of flexible work arrangements. It has helped companies to develop effective responses to the child-care needs of their employees. In the future, Catalyst hopes to continue to educate policymakers on women's career development, with advice on how to "break the glass ceiling." Thirty years ago, the workplace was the realm of men, and women were pretty much relegated to the home. How different the corporation is today, with women and men working together at all levels.

❧ II

In June 1992 we experienced one of our happiest moments. We were grateful to see our joint venture, Peggy, happily married to Robert Cornog. Later that year our good fortune would change. In the winter I traveled to Berlin with the Pitney-Bowes Board again. I was glad that my husband could share that experience with me. Berlin lost all of its grand luxury hotels during the bombing of World War II, but the East German government, eager for hard currency, had built several elegant new ones that met the best international standards. Tom and I checked into the Grand Hotel Esplanade, which opened in 1988 with superb facilities and impeccable service. Vintage Marlene Dietrich publicity shots lined the lobby of the Grand, which also exhibited works of Berlin's most acclaimed artists in one of its salons.

It excited us to see the proud capital city united after the divisive Wall was torn down. Germany has thrown its remarkable energies and resources into knitting this once-divided capital back into a grand world metropolis. Signs pointing motorists to the old Eastern sector say simply, "Mitte," indicating the center of the new central city created on October 3, 1990 when the East German regime disappeared. The long-neglected imperial museums, churches and palaces in the former East Berlin are being rehabilitated. On Unter-den-

Linden, once described as Berlin's Champs-Elysées, wartime bombing left huge gaps that were filled in hurriedly by blocks of unimpressive buildings erected by the Ulbricht and Honecker dictatorships for use as party secretariats and conference halls. The original linden trees were long ago destroyed by bombs or chopped down for fuel. A forest of construction cranes dominate that area where police watchtowers and the Wall once stood. (Enterprising entrepreneurs on every street corner were trying to sell us bits of masonry from the Wall.)

We visited the Reichstag, that imposing example of Prussian architecture built in the 1890s to house the Prussian Parliament. Thirty years later, it was occupied by the government of the ill-fated Weimar Republic until it burned to a shell under mysterious circumstances in 1933. (The Nazis blamed the Communists and used that as an excuse for suspending the Constitution.) Though the rebuilt Reichstag was badly damaged by bombs again in 1945, it is being reconstructed and will house the German Parliament when it moves from Bonn to Berlin. (New offices are being built in the area for members of the Bundestag and their staffs.)

I was eager to hear a performance of the world-renowned Berlin Philharmonic, but my husband wanted to rest instead of going with me. I started out alone to the Kammermusik-Saal, the new chamber music hall within the Philharmonic complex where the orchestra performed during the restorations. Tom was returning to the hotel lobby alone, when one of the heavy swinging doors blew shut. In a freak accident, he was knocked unconscious on the blue-marble floor of the foyer.

No one knew who Tom was at first, and he was in no condition to tell them. The manager called an ambulance that took him to the nearest hospital in the former East Zone, with antiquated facilities dating back to the days of the Iron Curtain. When he woke up, he discovered that his knee was smashed, and they were rushing him to the emergency operating room.

The scar on his knee still shows; the cut was at right angles to the injury, the *wrong* direction (according to the orthopedic surgeon we consulted back in the U.S.). The effect of the World War II-vintage anesthetic was the worst part; it left Tom groggy and confused for days.

You can imagine my shock and disbelief when I returned from the concert and found him gone. By this time the people at the desk realized the victim was my husband. They were kind and helpful, but it was too late to move him to a hospital in the American zone.

Tom spent a week in that former Iron Curtain facility, and those days were long ones for me. Arranging to get him back to the States for proper treatment as quickly as possible kept me busy. I visited Tom every evening at the hospital, a short walk from the hotel through almost-deserted back streets, whistling in the dark. I imagined that someone would appear out of the shadows to grab my purse and credit cards, but I was lucky.

Because of Tom's veteran status, I presumed he could be sent home on a military plane. But his injury wasn't service-related, so the Army could not help us. He was still confined to a wheel chair and in pain when we caught a Delta flight back to Dulles airport. We rushed him from there to George Washington University Hospital.

After several weeks, Tom was moved to a nursing home to continue his recuperation. Because the nurses were often busy, I took time out from the office to rush to the home twice a day to change the dressing on the wound. Long months of physical therapy at Fox-Chase Rehab Center on East-West Highway followed. This was one of my most stressful experiences. I had no idea what far-reaching consequences Tom's accident would have on my own life.

In 1984, Robert Strauss, a leading Democrat, had suggested my name to Senator Robert Dole as a top fund-raiser to head a foundation for the employment of people with disabilities. Dole, who has limited use of his right arm and partial use of his left hand as a result of World War II injuries, invited me to come aboard as a member of a non-partisan committee setting up the foundation. President George Bush appointed me to the board as an original member, and I eventually became treasurer of that organization.

The Dole Foundation was conceived as a way of stimulating grass-roots employment and training programs for people with handicaps, *any* handicap—including hearing and visual impairment. Paul G. Hearne, a highly intelligent and capable person, handicapped at birth and confined to a motorized wheelchair, was named president of the Foundation. Senator Dole brought Paul down from New York where he had headed J.O.B. ("Just One Break"), the first private job-placement agency in the U.S. for people with disabilities. It was organized as early as 1947 by Bernard Baruch, with the backing of Eleanor Roosevelt.

Julia with Senator Robert Dole.

Risks & Rewards

Our first objective at the Foundation was to lobby for the Americans with Disabilities Act (ADA), passed by Congress in July 1990. The Funding Partnership for People with Disabilities, a unique consortium comprised of 45 foundations and corporations, joined together to provide over $3 million in support of independent living and economic advancement for the disabled. In addition to grant programs and educational publications, videos and forums, we formed the Telecommunications Partnership for People with Disabilities, using the Funding Partnership as a model. This was based on the idea that people with disabilities should be in on the ground floor of the National Information Infrastructure.

By December 1994 the Finance Committee, under the guidance of Chairman Ted Kratovil and the Foundation staff, raised some $1,375,000 toward our year-end goal of $1.5 million. The Foundation already had awarded some 300 grants in 40 states.

It was my misfortune not to be able to celebrate its success. When I agreed to serve this worthy cause, I never expected that I would become one of the handicapped myself. In March 1993, a year after my husband's accident, I returned from the office one night, feeling more tired than usual. Throughout my life, whenever I've felt a cold coming on or some other minor illness, I have always comforted myself with a bowl of tomato soup. That night, I opened another can. I brought some work home with me, then stayed up to watch the late TV shows in the den. It was about one o'clock when I started to climb the stairs. Everything blacked out. I can't remember anything that happened until I awoke from a life-threatening coma at Sibley Hospital, with members of my family hovering over me.

Senator Dole immediately called Sibley when he heard, and as soon as I could receive visitors, Paul Hearne came by, bringing a handwritten letter from the Senator expressing his concern. Most of that spring and summer of 1993, I was undergoing physical therapy at the National Rehabilitation Center.

My Life's Greatest Challenge

My life's greatest challenge lay ahead, beating back from a major debilitating stroke. With God's help, I am sure I can lick it. I never realized how many friends I had until they sent flowers and messages that they were standing by with love and understanding.

That Christmas, Tom and I had much to be thankful for. We were both alive and had our wonderful family pulling for us. The photograph of another American President and his family in the Red Room of the White House was added to the collection in our den: "Our family wishes you and yours a joyful holiday season, and a New Year blessed with *health*, happiness, and peace," signed by Bill Clinton and his wife, Hillary Rodham Clinton.

Two years later, I was able to attend a White House reception in a wheelchair with other members of the American News Women's Club. This was the fifth First Lady I had the opportunity to meet: Democrats Eleanor Roosevelt, Lady Bird Johnson, Rosalyn Carter, and Hillary Clinton. As an honorary Smith College alumna, I was also photographed at the White House with a Republican President's wife, Barbara Bush. After taking tea with Mrs. Clinton and hearing her address our group, I was hopeful that she would follow in the footsteps of my idol, Mrs. Roosevelt, and that some of the programs she inspired would come to fruition.

In 1994 I was invited to attend the Sixth Annual Washington Business "Hall of Fame" at the Renaissance Hotel. I was to be honored as a "Laureate," along with business leaders Christian Heurich, Sr., Foster Shannon, of Shannon and Luchs, W. Reid Thompson, former CEO of PEPCO, and Earle C. Williams, former CEO of BDM International. Because of my health I couldn't make it, but my son Mark Montgomery spliced together a video presentation of the significant high points of my life so that I could "be there" anyway. Honorary Chairman and Master of Ceremonies Edward

F. Mitchell said some very nice things about me: "[Julia] is no longer active in the business, but her spirit remains strong in her sons, daughters, and associates. Walsh taught them to take risks, to put your reputation and your future on the line in an attempt to do something bigger and better'."

Today, most of the children have followed in my footsteps in the investment business. My only daughter, Peggy Walsh Cornog, is vice president of Fuji Capital, specializing in the derivatives market. John Montgomery, my oldest son, is chief investment strategist at Gibralter Advisors/ Prudential Securities. Michael Montgomery is chief financial officer at Goldman-Sachs (Canada). Stephen Montgomery is a broker with Raymond James, an investment company based in St. Petersburg, Florida. Mark Montgomery, my youngest, is a vice president at Tucker Anthony.

When Voice of America interviewer Chantal Mompoulian asked me, "What was the greatest joy in your life?" My answer was easy: my greatest satisfaction was in having married for the second time, in having this number of happy, well-adjusted children, and still having continued with my own career. As a grandmother of 15, I look back from the vantage point of a full and, for the most part, happy life to share some of the lessons I have learned with my family and future generations:

> *Work hard. Play hard.*
>
> *Put back into the community what you take from it.*
>
> *Obstacles are put in your path to be overcome.*
>
> *Women face many obstacles in a man's world, but with hard work and perseverance, these can be overcome.*
>
> *Whenever you can, go first class.*
>
> *It's a small, big world; see as much of it as you can.*

In the following chapter, I shall share some basic tips about how *you* can master the securities game.

CHAPTER NINE

Winning Positions For Women

OUR MOST IMPORTANT freedom, as women, is economic freedom: for a young woman to achieve independence, she must be *financially* independent. The securities industry offers many marvelous opportunities for women, today more than ever.

Yet many women aren't attracted to it because of the high risk and competition involved. The way girls are raised makes it difficult for them to compete. The women's movement and federal employment laws have helped, as have changing cultural attitudes. But hesitation and self doubt, not discrimination, are the high hurdles any woman must clear on her way to success.

There has always been a shortage of positive female role models, especially during my early years in the business. As a pioneer woman, I tried not to step on anyone's toes. On the few occasions I was invited into the smoke-filled, after-dinner discussion groups with industry veterans, I *listened*.

Communication between women brokers and their clients tends to be good because women are good listeners. I believe that investors, men or women, are more inclined to communicate their fears and ask questions of a woman than a male broker. Yet many women who aren't used to making financial decisions have been conditioned to go to men to manage their money. Conditioning can be a two-edged sword that cuts the woman broker off from women investors.

I see it changing in this generation, but women in my age group were not taught to ask for anything. If we went to a party, we were supposed to wait to be asked to dance. Many women found it hard to knock on someone's door and say, "Look, I've got a good service for you." They tended to wait until someone sought them out.

As a strategy to the woman broker hesitant to do the asking that will bring clients to her, I recommend that she gives lectures, teaches workshops and seminars, or anything else that allows her to show her knowledge to a group of potential clients. Joining a community, cultural, political or educational group can also help the woman broker. By making a contribution to the group, she will become known to people who will eventually seek her out. If you try to find a graceful way to encourage clients to give you referrals, that is a technique that can be lucrative in *any* business. Opportunities to be on radio or TV should be pursued. My connection with *Wall $treet Week With Louis Rukeyser* was just about the best thing that happened to me. It brought me into the homes of thousands of viewers who might be prospective clients. You might also offer to write columns for community newspapers to get in front of people.

Success in our business depends in part on what kinds of accounts a broker can attract. Men can move into a new community and have a lot of connections through old-school and club ties. Women generally don't have the same kinds of connections and opportunities that help develop a broad-based brokerage business. The industry was developed and brought about by men. Male dominance is built into it, and it's difficult for women to operate under those conditions.

Even today, many women face the frustration of never being included in the male fraternity. I still consider myself a fringe-member of the club, the old-boy network of brokers and investors grounded in school, family and fraternal ties. I don't belong to the old-line clubs of Washington such as the Metropolitan, bastion of lawyers and businessmen, or Burning Tree Country Club, whose membership is still open to men only. A lot of business goes on at the golf course. I don't play golf.

But I learned a lot in the early days by asking questions of male colleagues. What was it like during the Crash of 29? How did you survive World War II? In this volatile business, it's tough to see the market in relation to the bigger picture without historical perspective. Historically, women were left out almost entirely, but we are entering the mainstream and moving faster and faster.

Today, a woman can move more rapidly into the power structure by taking on problem-solving roles on boards and committees. One of the fallacies about women is that we can't get along together, can't work for a woman boss. In my view, that's a lot of malarkey! But along the way, it may help to find yourself a male mentor who happens to have a daughter. Men with daughters tend to be more supportive of other women.

Since men are more likely to grow up with knowledge of family finances, they may have more background when they enter the business. Firms must give women extra training, by sending them to school, conferences, lectures or wherever they can pick up the knowledge they need. Women need their confidence built up, their exposure increased and their ability to perform enhanced by the firm. Most firms haven't given much thought to how to build a woman broker's confidence and help to create opportunities for her.

Brokers new to the business are usually put on commission for six months after training. In my view, beginning brokers should be put on salary, not subject to the temporary fluctuations in the market. We brokers are suffering from what I call the "month-to-month syndrome." Every month you feel you have to start over and produce again, regardless of the market environment. This orients the broker to short-term goals, not to seeing the market with long-range perspective.

I also propose that new brokers act as account assistants to seasoned senior brokers for a year or two. The longer training period would make them more self-confident and better able to deal with the knowledge they have, once they are on their own.

No matter how successful the training program, I promise you it won't be easy. I worked 70 and 80 hours a week during the early years of my career. If a woman wants to be a successful broker, she must be willing to work harder than in any other industry. And she must find her own style, not try to copy her male counterpart. I get upset with women who feel that "getting to the top" means "becoming a white male," that being a corporate leader means dressing, acting, and thinking like a man. We women provide a balance that has been missing from the system. We are more humanistic, not as materialistic. We look at the social and human implications of a problem, whereas men tend to look solely at the bottom line.

As a mentor to young women MBA's coming out of the business schools, I offer this bottom-line advice to those trying to break into this select club:

> *Get a strong education in economics, take a course in accounting, attend an investment seminar.*
>
> *Learn to evaluate, to understand the market, to take risks. (During 1978, when I had a lot at stake in real*

estate and energy, I took great losses, but surviving
this gave me confidence to risk it all again.)

Go for leadership roles in organizations, do volunteer
work; get involved with the problem-solving bodies
that mold the industry. The way to be a leader is to
solve problems.

Don't evaluate today's economy by the last decade's
rules. Look to future fields, such as high-tech and
energy. That's where the action is.

There is plenty of room in the financial field for any young woman with persistence, dedication and plain hard work. The talents you bring to this arena, the contributions you can make, are just beginning. We're the only Western nation that's tapping into our women power, so this doubles our prospects in the international market.

❧ II

Women have been duped into thinking they control the wealth in this country. The truth is, many women inherited that wealth, and it's not controlled by them. We have little to say about the direction of that wealth. It's time we set about handling our own business affairs. It's time to plan, consolidate our assets, use our resources intelligently, and gain experience by doing.

Until the 1970s, about 80 percent of my clients at Ferris & Company were men. The proportion of women rose steadily, however, and by the time of my retirement more than half of my accounts were controlled by women. Still, too many women are letting their husbands or fathers or even sons take care of them. But if they are widowed or divorced, and suddenly are left alone, what do they do with their money? Women must take hold of their own lives and manage their own money; they can't allow emotionalism to prevent them from thinking rationally. I've seen hysterical responses from too many educated women when it comes to handling money.

The first thing a woman should do is to get a basic knowledge of what's going on in the investment arena, what's available, what the rewards are, what the problems are. Then she must examine her own financial assets, determine her own objectives, and begin managing her own money. Even today, social conditioning has left many women unable to handle their financial affairs. I believe that a woman should not only handle her own money but should feel comfortable in being an *aggressive* investor if she wants to be.

We've been taught, in our conditioning, to be safe—not to take risks. But we have to examine what a great risk it is to live a risk-less kind of life. If you really want to be *risk-less*, that's pretty *reckless*. Even in difficult periods, if you take an intelligent, conscientious approach to the market, it's the best place to be. Real estate, while also a fast-appreciating investment, requires *more* risk and *more* hands-on commitment.

Understanding how the economy works involves a process not unlike choosing a career. You need to look at the world and say, where do my opportunities lie? For example, if they lie in the field of communication, where are those opportunities the greatest? In satellites, in broadcasting companies, in the new high-tech means of transmission, in telephone-switching systems? Go from the areas of greatest opportunity to segments of that area and identify those segments with the greatest amount of potential. In the 60s, it was the computer industry. In the 70s, it was energy. In the 80s, it was personal computers, telecommunications equipment and semi-conductors.

It should be part of a woman's life to think in terms of maximizing her assets. It's part of a man's thinking to build his financial future as he goes along. He's conditioned to it. Women generally are not. It's disappointing that they haven't focused more on this area. In addition to not being adventurous, they are not being realistic. The principal difference in the way men and women invest is that men are much more inclined to take chances. Women more often settle for something they believe will offer more stability and security. Sometimes the things they think are secure can be riskier than the things that offer more opportunity. For example, women who invested in bonds in the late 1970s and early 1980s have seen this supposedly secure investment decrease dramatically in value. Then, just when everyone felt that inflation was a fact of life, the bond market had its best decade in terms of total return on record.

I'm very much more in favor of equity securities, and reinvesting dividends. There are also mutual funds. These are the only ways that a woman with limited assets can get ahead. To win at the market game, the woman investor must put her money where the new growth is going to be. My strategy calls for buying two or three of the best prospects within a favored industry, with the expectation that one will hold its own or decline, one will do fairly well, and one will be sensational. A long range investment is now considered three to five years. Investors who want to make money can't afford to have a sentimental attachment to an old favorite stock. Fall in love with people, fall in love with causes, but never fall in love with an investment. In the decade of the 90s, I'm betting on high-technology.

My advice is to look at the world around you and identify areas that you think could be interesting. For instance, look at the company you work for. When you find something you think is promising, read up on it. Anyone who wants to be an intelligent investor has to be a *current* investor. That means keeping up with change on the economic scene. Learn all you can about corporate performance, growth potential, the company's position in the marketplace and general economic trends.

Take a course in investing. It's worth the time and effort. Women—as CEOs of the most important economic unit of all, the family—can be the wisest of all investors, because they understand the spending habits of the American buying public. I think that any woman can enter the market with only $10,000, even today, and start to build from there, as I did. My investment philosophy might be described as prudent risk-taking. That means looking for good stock buys where the downside risk is minimal and the potential for capital gains is large. When the risks seem low, and the possible rewards are great, that's when I buy.

This form of investing takes more skill than it used to. In the trade, we call these "second-tier" stocks, meaning those that are below the "gilt-edged" big-name corporations, but are still high-quality investments. Specifically, in 1996 I would look for bargains among utilities and specialty stocks related to energy and high-tech, especially among secondary issues.

In the beginning, I was a small—and inexperienced—investor myself. When John Montgomery and I returned to the States from our overseas assignment, we had saved $2,000 to spend on a new car. We decided to invest that amount in a solid stock, and if we lost, we would still have the old car to drive to work in. As told earlier, I took the $2,000 and bought shares of Goodyear Tire & Rubber, the hometown company that had been good to my family. The stock climbed from $25 a share to $50 within a very short time, and doubled our money. I have followed this strategy throughout my career—often for higher stakes—with amazing results.

From the beginning, I was sold on equities, but safe and sure ones. After attending the Harvard program, I set my sights higher and moved into more dramatic areas—the riskier, high-tech stocks that paid for my house. If this is a good investment strategy for a man, why can't a woman achieve that level, too? And it doesn't make sense to maintain the traditional portfolio of 20 years ago. No longer can you buy a stock and stay with it forever. The market today is much more specialized. My advice to the new investor is to buy selectively, keep some good solid cash in reserve, but make sure you're protected against inflation. I feel very strongly that a well-directed, well-thought-out investment program in equities is, and always has been, the place to be. But it is very important to look at the long-term, rather than the short-term, cycles of the market.

In spite of today's higher salaries and growth in disposable income, many women are still content to stash their money away in a joint checking account or at the savings and loan institutions with their husbands, without giving a thought to such important considerations as whether they should have separate bank accounts for tax purposes. In the event that they are widowed or divorced, women should keep up-to-date on their financial situation. They should study the market and make their own decisions. There is little excuse to remain ignorant or uninvolved. There is a whole, new financial world out there waiting to be conquered, or at least considered; things such as tax shelters, mutual funds, real estate investments, equity plans and retirement funds. In my view, the best tax shelter today is a long-term capital gain.

What advice do I have to offer the young woman with a nest egg of $10,000 today? The following are three important steps for the beginning investor that have guided my own decisions:

> *Assess your present position, then compare the value of your investments every quarter against an economic yardstick, such as Standard & Poor's or the Consumer Price Index. Then ask yourself, what is my long-term goal? To preserve capital? Buy bonds. To increase capital? Buy stocks. Then take into account the risk factor. How much risk can you tolerate? But remember that*

*the safest investors in the last few years did the worst,
those who were invested in long-term bonds.*

*The Rule of 10. If you're in securities, never own more
than 10, because beyond about 10 or 15, no one can
really keep track and you'll be over-diversified. Don't
buy a new security unless you sell one.*

*Deciding where to invest. This involves homework,
and perhaps a trusted adviser to discuss things with.
Then, look at what changes are taking place in
the market and what companies are meeting those
changes realistically.*

In the next decade, management-labor relations will be
one of the important factors in selecting a stock. Being in the
right *area* is another consideration; to be at the right point in
the development of an industry. For example, I began to make
my fortune when the country was moving toward computeri-
zation and high-technology, and I invested wisely in those
companies. (I see financial services, health, and high-tech as
growth areas today.) But most important, stay with a stock
only as long as you think it is a good investment. You can't just
put your money away and forget it. You have to pay constant
attention to the market. Being passive about money is the
worst mistake a woman can make. My advice to any woman:
learn how money works, then handle some on your own.
Save your money, then invest in something—even if only a few
shares per month of a mutual fund. Learn, and from that
knowledge, build.

If this successful investment strategy allowed me to parlay
a small nest egg into a multi-million dollar fortune, it can work
for you, too.

III

In viewing the changing roles of women in today's world, I see the Hillary Rodham Clinton generation assuming positions of power in government and in business. Over half of my life was lived before women had such opportunities.

As I look back, there were several recurring themes that contributed to my success. Early in the game, I taught myself to be more at home in the stock market than in the supermarket. Any other young woman, with as little experience as I had, can do it, too. This is my personal "grocery list" of attitudes to cultivate for those who hope to follow in my path:

Julia meeting with another First Lady Hillary Rodham Clinton.

Winning Positions For Women

Practice risk-taking: to me, it's like putting nickels in the slot machine, if you don't put any in, you don't have a chance to win.

Get as much education in your chosen field as you can, then keep focused on your career, in spite of changes in your personal life, e.g., marriage, children, divorce, widowhood. (I always kept working, even when my husband was posted to Turkey, a country with a different culture and language.)

Watch your health; high energy helps.

Don't waste emotional energy: anger, for instance, is a tiring experience. (Use the source of that anger as an accelerated career push, as I did after my first husband's death.)

Practice thinking objectively: What do I need to make my life work?

Take a cue from the way men have always operated: "When you get hit, you just go faster." Cultivate mentors in corporate life, buddies among male classmates.

Be flexible, able to shift gears and keep your own balance.

Play fair-and-square in your dealings with others (e.g., my mother-in-law was a full "partner"); there is also something to be said in favor of strong "family values."

Keep an optimistic outlook; it never helps to look back with regrets.

Today, women should focus on new undertakings on the wider, international scene, such as my work on the board of the Czecho-slovak American Enterprise Fund. It is important for women to get into the policy-setting and decision-making bodies of this country, to keep an eye on meaningful positions in the public-service sector. Whatever the future holds, I hope to continue to be a mentor and guide to a new generation of women.

Julia Montgomery Walsh in front of the United States Treasury Building.

Winning Positions For Women

Acknowledgments

In addition to Julia Montgomery Walsh's personal and public relations files, letters, and memorabilia, this book is indebted to many periodical sources, with special credit to: *The Washington Post, The New York Times, Wall Street Journal, Nation's Business, U.S. News and World Report, Life, Regardie's, Washingtonian, Los Angeles Times, Business Review of Washington, Dossier* (Washington), and *Anvil* (Wharton Alumni Magazine).

Gail Sheehy's *Pathfinders: Overcoming the Crises of Adult Life and Finding Your Own Path to Well-Being* (New York: William Morrow & Co., 1981), profiled Julia Montgomery Walsh as a "pathfinder."

Among the many friends and colleagues who contributed their personal anecdotes and recollections:

Louis Rukeyser of *Wall $treet Week With Louis Rukeyser*; Paul G. Hearne, president of the Dole Foundation; Dr. Victor Li, former president of East-West Center, Honolulu; Jane Wyman, administrative assistant, Julia Walsh & Sons; Jane Prentice, administrative assistant, Julia Walsh & Sons; Beth Wainwright, stock broker; Jeanne Beekhuis, principal of Beekhuis & Co.; Sari Barbas, lifelong friend;

Amy Williams, JMW's strong-right-arm at home for some
30 years; stepdaughter Joan Walsh Cassedy; and Elizabeth
(Beth) Koehler Montgomery, Stephen's wife.

With special gratitude to:
John Montgomery, who reviewed the manuscript twice and
offered his advice and expertise in the world of business;
Mark, Stephen, and Michael Montgomery, the other "Sons"
who made this book possible; Margaret Elizabeth ("Peggy, Jr.")
Walsh, Julia's only daughter; and Thomas M. Walsh, former
vice chairman of National Permanent Federal Savings & Loan,
Julia's devoted husband.

Thanks also to Judith H. Quattlebaum, who provided
the quiet retreat on Chesapeake Bay where the memior was
finished.

A.C.C.

Index

Index

Anne Conover Carson

ANNE CONOVER CARSON, who has lived most of her life in or near Washington, D.C., went west to gain her BA and MA at Stanford University. She was an editor at John Hopkins University Press and the Hispanic Division, Library of Congress, before joining the U.S. Information Agency. There she was staff editor/writer of *Problemas Internacionales* and *Book Scene,* publications circulated to more than 1,000 USIA posts around the world. She has written biographies of two other outstanding women, Caresse Crosby and Olga Rudge.